Needle Felting

A Complete Course

From Beginner to Advanced with Step-by-Step Instructions

Lori Rea

This needle felting adventure is
dedicated to my grandmother

Dorothy

Teacher of art
and nurturer of dreams

Acknowledgments

My Mother
The cheerleader

My Husband
The believer

My Brother
The advisor

Marissa, Sarah and Kaela
The supporters

Chuck Sr., Ryan, Daniel and Ben
The marketers

Benjamin, Richard and Ellie
The three littles

Hope
The influencer

First published in the United States of America by Lori Rea

ISBN: 978-1-7343141-0-6

www.naturecrafty.com

Contents

Needle Felting

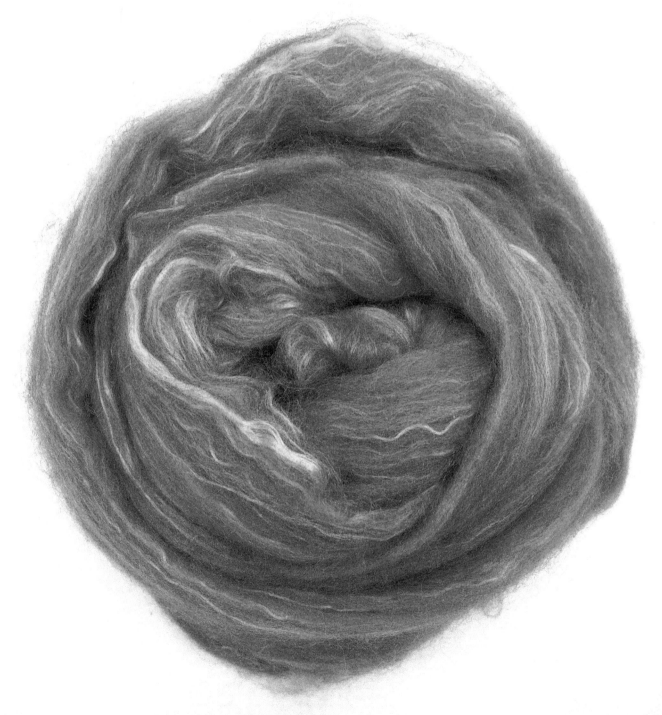

Introduction

Most people are truly amazed the first time they see a wool sculpture created by needle felting. If you are reading this book, it means that you are at least somewhat curious about the process of how a pile of wool can turn into such amazing works of art. This book will demystify the needle felting process and give you the skills and inspiration to begin your own artistic felting journey.

Needle felting is the newest, up-and-coming fiber art in the world. If the traditional fiber arts were a family, needle felting would be the free-spirited, trend setting relative that somewhat recently married into the clan. Needle felting is bringing revitalized energy into the world of wool arts much like the way that Kate Middleton and Meghan Markle have revitalized the royal family with fresh energy and spirit. Needle felting is the hottest new commodity in the fiber community.

When I started needle felting in 2012, there were few Youtube videos, books or blogs to help me learn this mysterious new art. Presently there is a plethora of videos and blogs with tutorials for specific projects, but there is very little sequential instruction available for the beginner. This book is for those who want to have a learning experience that walks them through the entire process: understanding wool and tools, moving on to simple projects (designed to help you learn the basic techniques) all the way through to armatures and more complicated and realistic pieces.

Needle felting can be a challenging subject matter to teach via any media because it's unlike the other fiber crafts that use patterns and counting. Needle felting is sculpting with loose wool which makes it more of a free-form art. Learning how to needle felt is not complicated, but it does take patience and practice.

Enjoy the journey and process of needle felting. Your projects will start out simply and they won't be perfect but as you progress you will improve. As time passes you will develop your own style and eventually you will no longer need a guide, you will be able to study a photograph of a real animal or object and create your own piece.

Stay in touch

For new tutorials, book giveaways and current videos go to www.naturecrafty.com and sign up for our monthly newsletter.

WHAT IS NEEDLE FELTING?

Needle felting is the process of turning wool into felt by the use of a specialized needle. This sharp, notched needle tangles and locks the wool fibers together as it is stabbed into the wool.

The History of Needle felting

Humans have been utilizing wool and its superior properties since ancient times. Wet felting or fulling has been used for thousands of years to make clothing, bed clothes, tents, saddle bags and a myriad of other useful items.

Needle felting needles for machines were invented in the 1860's as a method to produce felt fabric without water. Industrial felt is widely used in many kinds of products: mattresses, clothing, car carpets and other applications.

The countries with the highest needle felting population include: The US, UK, New Zealand, Japan and Russia.

The areas with the greatest amount of felters in the USA are Oregon, Washington, New England, California and Wisconsin.

The Waldorf educational movement, with its emphasis on natural materials in art, deserves an honorable mention in the history of needle felting as they were some of the first to promote wool crafts and felting.

History Makers

Needle felting as a craft started in the 1980's when Eleanor and David Stanwood took industrial felting needles from a machine and began to use them to make sculptures out of wool. They transformed needle felting from a industrial process to a handcrafted art form.

Two more early pioneers: Ayala Talpai in the US and Brigitte Hansen from Denmark, furthered the craft with workshops and the first felting books.

Needle felting started gaining a wider audience as the world wide web started to expand and more artists began to blog, post pictures and teach on You tube.

Today, there are many teachers and brilliant artists leading the needle felting movement. Throughout this book I've highlighted a few of the many that are in the forefront of this fiber craft. In the USA, Sara Renzulli and Marie Spaulding both have had a huge influence. The explosive growth of this new fiber craft came, in part, through the generous teaching efforts of these two women on You tube and their informative websites devoted to selling to felters specifically.

10

11

www.Sarafinafiberart.com

Sara Renzulli is a pioneer in the art of needle felting. She is famous for her YouTube teaching videos and is the owner of a thriving needle felting shop and online business: Sarafina Fiber Art - located in Elkton, Maryland. She has been an innovative inventor of tools for needle felting and is credited with coining many needle felting terms.

When I first met Sara I was struck by two things: her friendly, calm vibe and her wit. This energy flows throughout her creations and her shop. Sara takes her art and her business seriously but also enjoys sprinkling playful touches of whimsy throughout everything she does.

Sara's needle felting style is relaxed and her work is full of expression. Her sculptures are on the softer side and have charming character. She's an animal enthusiast that is dedicated to capturing the true nature of her subjects. Her goal is not perfect realism and a super-firm sculpture, but rather she believes that interpreting an animal as your eyes see it, will bring out its most life-like qualities.

Sara began her needle felting career by selling sculptures but quickly transitioned to selling kits and wool after seeing the need for a retailer solely devoted to felting. Her business now serves both US and international felters. Sustainability is important to Sara and she strives to source her wool ethically and endeavors to keep her business as green and eco-friendly as possible.

Sara's Inventions:

Stabbit Wabbit - a burlap, rice filled bag for stabbing - eco-friendly
Zulli tool - Helps create consistent shapes of various sizes
Digitwidget - For consistently sized fingers, toes, limbs
Swax - An original formula, it both smooths and firms wool and makes beaks, toes and horns

Advice: Enjoy the process of learning, be patient with yourself and don't fall into the trap of comparison with what others are doing. Take time to fall in love with the wool and the act of stabbing to create something beautiful. **Technique:** Wrapping an armature is an important skill to master. Practice and learn it well as it cuts down on felting time.

A visit to Sarafina Fiber Art is both exciting and comforting, like going to visit a good friend. As you enter Sara's magical wool emporium, you are welcomed by friendly employees and an enthusiastic dog named Milo. Sarafina's has a relaxed mood and an eclectic approach. The entry includes a vintage couch, books and a variety of art and finished sculptures. As you wander further on, there are huge, prismatic displays of every kind of wool, and in every color, flowing out of bins and baskets. Sara hosts her world-famous workshops right in her shop and the attendees get to spend time learning, making friends and enjoying the gorgeous countryside where Sarafina Fiber Art is located.

Wool

Wool

Wool is an amazing material, versatile in its uses and ancient in its history. The properties of wool are unrivaled by any man-made substance; it insulates against both heat and cold, is fire resistant and has antibacterial properties. Wool derives from many different animals but for the needle felter, sheep wool is the gold standard.

When wool comes off the sheep in the form of a fleece, it is first picked through to remove vegetable matter, then it is sent to a mill where it is scoured (washed gently).

The quality of the wool fleece is evaluated and the fineness and length of the fiber (staple) will determine how the wool is processed in the next step.

Wool is generally sold or processed in a few different ways: cleaned fleece, locks, batt, roving or combed top.

If you are a felter, you need to understand wool, its properties (how it behaves) and how it is processed. The success of your project depends on choosing the right wool product for the piece you wish to create. The needs of needle felters are unique among fiber artists and a bit of wooly education will save you both time and money.

"A lot of people believe that wool is just wool. But there are huge differences in breeds and individual sheep.

There are over 200 breeds of sheep in the world. Each and every one of those sheep, not just the breeds, have different micron counts. There is no bad wool, just wool for different purposes. Merino wool is well known for its softness. There are other fine wools as well..The further the scales are apart, the more it begins to look like what we think of as hair. The Karakul breed is a good example, it's coarse and is great for rug making because it can stand up to a lot of wear."

Lavonne Stucky, Gallatin Valley sheep farmer (30 years)
The wool Mill on Facebook and Instagram

''The rougher the wool feels and the higher the micron count, the quicker it will felt...but the rougher the final surface will be. In the same way, the smoother the wool feels (repeatedly carded wool tops, for example) and the lower the micron count number, the slower it will felt and the finer the final surface will be. This is why many felters use a core wool...core wool is rough but inexpensive''

Clare Lepetit, veteran needle felter, France.

Choose Your Wool Carefully

As a new felter, full of premature confidence and wishful thinking, I set about buying wool from various websites displaying their colorful assemblages. I had no understanding of the differences in fiber processing but I put color after color into my shopping cart with abandon - anything that struck a chord in my artistic spirit. I mostly chose combed top because it was so vibrant and colorful. When the wool was finally delivered to my door, I unboxed it and squealed like a child in a candy store. The colors were so vibrant and beautiful! I was in wool heaven and knew I would be the queen of everything felted. After spending ridiculous amounts of time staring at it all, I set about trying to make my envisioned ten inch tangerine colored heart to hang on my wall.

I took the silky, tangerine combed top and started to felt. I stabbed for what seemed like hours yet my project remained flat and limp. The heart was nothing like what I had imagined! I was so confused.

I didn't realize I had picked the incorrect wool product for my project. I had chosen badly and my heart was, quite literally, a flop.

If I had only known then what I know now, I would have made the base of my heart out of batt and it would have felted up quickly with a firm core. The combed top color would have been added on as a finishing touch. So, with that little failure story in mind, please take heed and study the following pages on wool/fiber processing so you don't waste time and money buying the wrong fiber product.

Locks

Combed Top

Roving

Batt

Wool Processing

Types of Processed Wool

After the sheep is sheared, the fleece is then washed and the processing begins. As needle felters, we mainly concern ourselves with the following types of processed wool: batt, roving, combed top and locks.

Locks

Locks are the curly or crimped looking part of the fleece that has been washed but not processed. They are fun to add to projects for visual interest and are used for finishing touches. You can purchase them in both natural and dyed colors.

• Great for sheep coats, dolls hair or Santa beards
• Incorporated into wall hangings and abstract pieces
• Used to add texture and visual interest

Combed Top

Combed top, or Top for short, is created by combing the fibers in the same direction with much of the space between the fibers being eliminated. It has a smooth, silky sheen to its appearance. It is sold in ropes and comes is a huge variety of colors. Don't try to make the core of your project with top, it doesn't felt up firmly.

• Characteristics: silky, wispy, long fibers
• Great for wool paintings
• Wet felting - it is soft against the skin
• Finishing touches and outlining
• Smooth top finish with sheen

Roving

Roving is sold in rope form. It is very similar to batt in that its fibers are going in different directions and it felts up firm and fast. Roving is removed from the drum carder in ropes, with a slight twist as it comes off the carder. Roving is good for anything that needs to be wrapped, like armatures or balls. Some people use the term roving and top interchangeably, but true roving is more coarse than top.

• Felts up firmly and quickly
• Color blending is easy

Batt

Batt is a carded wool and is sometimes known as **core** wool. It is produced by putting the washed fleeces on a machine called a drum carder. When wool comes off the carder in sheets, it is fluffy in appearance and the fibers are flowing in multiple directions. Batt is the backbone of needle felting. It is used as the base or core for almost all projects as it felts up quickly and firmly. Most felters keep a few pounds of natural colored (undyed) core batt on hand at all times.

• Felts up firmly and quickly with a smooth finish
• Core or base for most projects
• Good for color blending different colors together
• Works well for both 2-D and 3-D projects

Remember how to use the different types of processed wool by thinking of a cake.

Batt or roving is the cake middle, combed top is the icing and locks are the decorations.

Sheep

There are over 200 breeds of sheep and depending on the part of the world you live in, there will be a few breeds that are more dominant in terms of wool available in your region. Below, I have listed just a few of the more common breeds used for needle felting in the US.

The fibers of certain breeds are more suited to needle felting. If you have knowledge of the breeds and an understanding of their fiber quality your projects will be more successful. However, acquiring this knowledge takes time and experimentation. For your first orders of wool, I strongly suggest that new felters stick with buying from shops and businesses that tailor their products specifically to needle felters.

It is very challenging to recommend a certain breed of sheep to a worldwide audience but you can sleuth your local breeds yourself. Try to get to know the dominant sheep breeds in your geographical area by talking to other fiber artists (spinners, knitters) about their favorite wools and the farms they come from. Visit farms and sheep festivals, talk to the farmers and support them by using wool local to your area if possible.

Merino is generally considered a fine wool. It is soft and it is sold both as a single breed and as a mixed wool product. It does have a reputation for taking longer to felt up and it is not always firm when finished. It works well for wet felting (soft against the skin) and for adding detail and color to pieces. Not always a good choice for core wool, Merino is used mainly to cover over the base of a piece as a top coat.

Corriedale is a medium fine wool, it is a common choice of wool to blend with other breeds to produce a product that felts up firm and smooth.

Blue Faced Leicester is a long fine wool that has a lovely soft feel to it. It is not a fast felting wool but it does have a nice firmness to it when finished. Locks from this breed are beautiful.

Shetland is a fine wool with just a bit more bulk and crimp to it than merino but depending on the sheep, it can also contain annoying small hairs that do not felt down well. It is readily available and comes in beautiful natural colors.

Romney is a medium to coarse wool that felts nicely, has good spring and is a favorite of many.

Non-Sheep Fibers

Photo courtesy @Laughingcrowco

Alpaca is a very soft, fine fiber. In needle felting it is usually only used as a top coat. It's a fiber that doesn't felt down flat very well but it lends a super soft and silky quality as a top coat. It feels like little clouds under your fingers when you work with it.

Angora Goats give us mohair fiber. These long, curly coated goats are prized for their beautiful silky locks. The locks can be difficult to felt down as they are more slippery than sheep's locks but they are exquisite and worth the challenge.

Exotic fibers are fun to felt with and each have very distinct properties. It can be exciting to tryout different animal wool and fur. Some unique felting species might include: angora rabbit, bison, dog, cat, camel or yak. Your locale will determine what is available to you in terms of exotic fibers. Using these fibers in the right applications takes experimentation, so order sparingly to start.

Alternative Fibers

The non-animal fibers can be a bit more challenging to needle felt with at first but some artists have been very successful with both synthetic and plant based fibers.

Polyester stuffing or **Acrylic** can be used as a core for projects and it felts up quickly and very firmly. Once felted, it has very little spring to it.
Cotton, ramie, flax and hemp will felt but it can take a very long time to make them firm.
Banana, Rose and milk fiber are silky soft and hard to felt with but they can be added to the tops of projects.

Marie Spaulding

www.feltingsupplies.livingfelt.com
Facebook: Living Felt

When starting a new project, pick something that really speaks to you so that you are inspired to actually finish it.

Get close up and intimate with your work. Use good lighting so you can see clearly.

Learn what it's like to felt something very firmly in the beginning. If you don't like the firmly felted style, that's okay but know what it takes to get there.

Attend workshops if you can, the hands on experience is priceless.

Most of all, HAVE FUN! Enjoy the creative process.

Marie Spaulding is a friendly, creative spirit with a passion for felting and sharing. She is a gifted teacher with many videos on Youtube and her live felting demos (Wooly Wednesdays on Facebook) are extremely popular. Marie owns Living Felt, an online and brick and mortar shop in Austin, Texas that specializes in fiber for both needle and wet felters.

An accomplished felter, Marie has been both wet and needle felting since 2000. Her pieces are beautiful, colorful and fun. Marie believes that the process of felting should be pleasurable and that there is joy in creating something new. For Marie, personal expression in the art is what is important, not perfect realism. She encourages felters to experiment to find their unique style and to not worry about following prescribed methods but to embrace the freedom to forge a new path.

The Living Felt business started with published booklets on how to felt and soon afterward kits were created and products added as customers requested them. As Living Felt continued to prosper, it quickly outgrew its suppliers and Marie decided to not only source their own wool (from US farms) but also to develop a wool product that was superior for felting, both needle and wet. Their wool is now world famous. Living Felt also has a great variety of tools, kits and accessories. Marie has a high degree of commitment to keeping Living Felt as eco-friendly as possible and sustainability is a guiding belief in the development and sales of all of their products.

Living Felt holds many yearly, well attended workshops at their spacious shop with famous guest felting artists. Marie calls the workshops "rich experiences" where life-long friendships are made

and new skills can be cultivated and practiced.

Tools and Techniques

Needle Types

The magic of needle felting is made possible through the unique way felting needles are constructed. Felting needles are not like ordinary smooth sewing needles; they are different in that have tiny notches cut into the steel that go part way up their shaft. These tiny sharp notches, when poked into fiber, tangle and mat the fiber together and make the wool firm, or felted.

When choosing felting needles there are two major factors to consider: type and gauge. Type refers to the style of the needle and the number of barbs (and their placement) and gauge refers to the needles size and its ability to felt quickly or to do finer work.

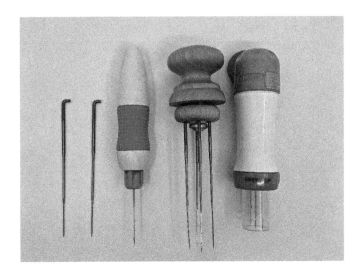

If you are just starting out, the recommendation I give to beginners is to purchase a **triangle blade in a #38.** This is the best all-purpose needle available. The minimum to start is three needles but a dozen is better.

Needle Types

Triangle blade needles - A triangle needle has three sides, typically with two barbs per side. Triangle needles are the most common needle type and come in the most variety of gauges. They are used for both sculptural and 2-dimensional needle felting. This is the best all purpose needle.

Star blade needles - A star felting needle has 4 sides, typically with two barbs per side. Because they have 4 sides, they have a little more power behind them to push more wool in with each stab as compared to a triangle needle. They are great for all purpose felting.

Spiral blade needles - A spiral (or twisted) felting needle is the same as a triangle needle, except that the blade is twisted. Instead of the barbs being located on three sides, they are evenly spaced as they corkscrew up the blade. Spiral-shaped needles leave less noticeable needle marks when compared to the same size needle in a triangle or star design and are therefore better for fine work.

Reverse (inverted) needles - A reverse/inverted barb needle works by pulling fibers **out** of the project rather than pushing them inward. Instead of catching and pushing fibers in as you poke downward, this needle will pull fiber out of your project as you withdraw it. Reverse needles are great for creating fuzzy finishes for animal fur.

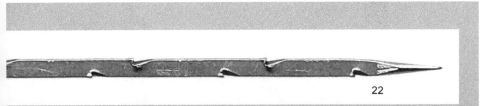

Close up of notches in a felting needle

Needle Gauge

Felting needles are sized by their diameter or "gauge" - meaning size. The gauge of a needle is an important factor in the felting process. Generally needle felters use gauges from #32 to #42. The lower number being the thicker needle for felting quickly (but leaving holes visible) and a higher number would be a thinner needle for fine work (and leaves less obvious holes).

#32 Gauge – This is a sturdy needle good for felting a piece up quickly. This is useful when you are making the core or base of the project. It felts wool up fast and firm and the needle holds up to intense stabbing better than the finer gauges. This gauge will leave larger needle marks in the surface so it's not ideal for top coat or fine work.

#36 Gauge – This needle is also good needle for core work. Similar to the #32, it will also leave some holes in the surface. Good for attaching pieces together.

Keep track of needle gauge by color-coating The tops of the needles with various colors of nail polish.

#38 Gauge – This is my all-around favorite needle. You can use it for both core work and some finer details. If you only have ONE needle make sure it's a #38. It can handle the largest variety of felting scenarios.

#40 Gauge – This is fine needle for detail work and getting a smooth surface. It is not intended for working with coarse fibers or firming up the core of a piece. This needle is great for adding on a top coat to an animal or for 2-D pieces that are more delicate.

#42 Gauge – A thin needle that is generally reserved for adding fine hair, tiny wisps of wool and thin, outlined details.

Core Work
fast felting
= Low Gauge
#32 - #38

Fine Finish
Smoothing Tops
= High Gauge
#38 - #42

Needles are delicate and they break easily. Please see the basic techniques section for information on the proper way to use your needle. Needles become blunt with use and may need to be replaced. You should always have at least 3 needles on hand for every piece you make.

Tools and Handy things

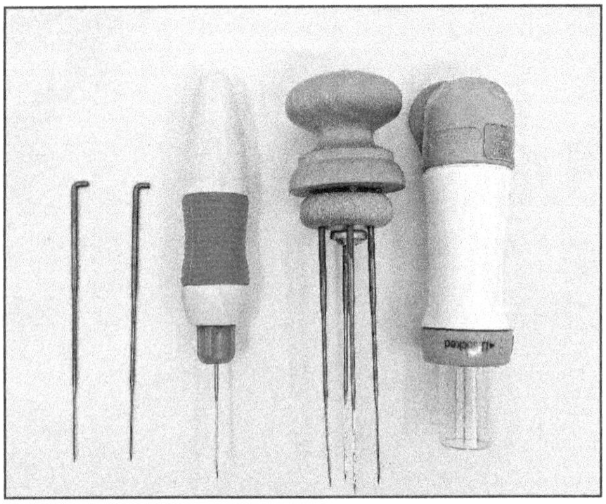

Needle holders are handy devices that save on wear and tear for your hands and wrists. It takes less energy to hold an ergonomic tool than a tiny needle. Needle holders range in capacity from 1 needle up to 12. Holders are optional but very helpful.

Larger projects almost certainly need a multi-needle holder but you can also tape up to 3 needles together for more punching power. You can shave 50% off of your total felting time with a multi-needle tool!

Keep in mind that these multi holders can also be weapons of mass destruction when you miss your project and stab yourself! Be careful.

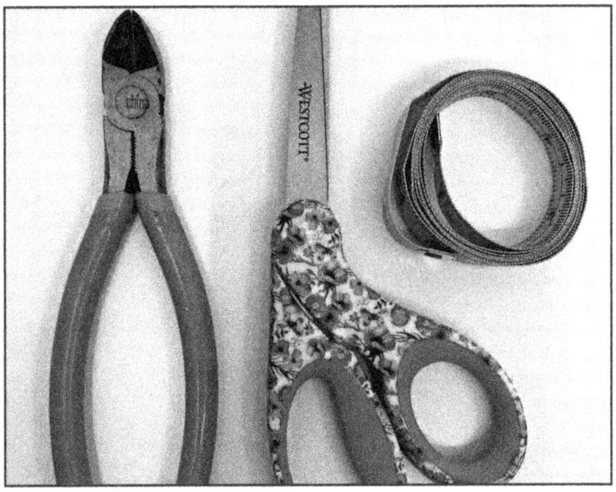

Pliers are necessary for cutting wire while making armatures.

Scissors are useful for trimming wool and cutting locks and wool to size (although tearing wool with the hands is generally a better practice)

Measuring tapes are very important when you are making a 3-D sculpture and need to get the correct proportions.

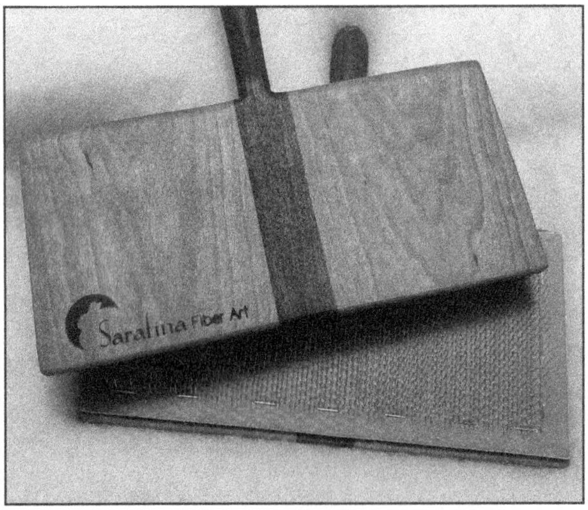

Hand carders from Sarafina Fiber Art (see resources)

Hand Carders and Dog Brushes - Hand carders make quick work of blending batt or roving together to make a new color and they are easy to use. However, you can also use dog brushes as they are the inexpensive, smaller version and work well for small color batches.

Finger guards are highly recommended for children or those that hate the sight of blood. They come in leather and silicone.

Wire for armatures in a variety of gauges. #18 gauge for large pieces and a #22 gauge for smaller projects. Galvanized wire or florist wire both work well.

Chenille stems/pipe cleaners are great and handy for all kinds of armatures or appendages for your projects. They are easy to wrap and readily available.

Needle Felting Surfaces

Felting needles are both sharp and fragile. To protect yourself and your work area you will need a firm pad to work on. There are several types of pads available: foam, brush pads, rice filled fabric bags and wool pads. My personal favorite is foam (always use eco-foam without fire retardant chemicals) but rice pads and brushes work well too.

Foam pads are the most popular felting surface. Always buy new foam pads and ask if they are free from chemical fire retardants. Living Felt (see resources) in the US makes a good eco-foam that is safe for use by felters.

Rice bags are simple and can be made or purchased. Sarafina Fiber Art makes and sells burlap/rice bags. Rice filled bags are an eco-friendly choice but they may not last as long as foam.

Wool mats are eco-friendly and work surprisingly well. It might seem crazy to felt on top of wool as you would think that your project would get stuck to the pad, but these mats are densely felted and projects rarely stick to them. The pads are usually on the smaller side so they don't work as well for large pieces.

Brushes for needle felting can be found in most major craft stores. Brushes are small and only work for small items.

Toxic Foam

For many years the upholstery foam used in furniture making had fire-retardant chemicals added to it. These chemicals may have cancer causing properties and when the foam is stabbed repeatedly, dust is created and can be inhaled into the lungs.
NEVER use upholstery foam for felting unless you are sure it is free from fire-retardants.

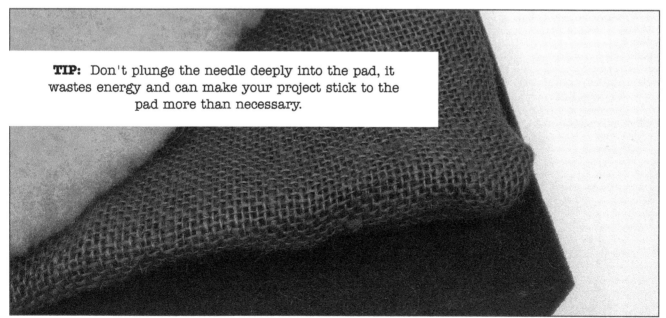

TIP: Don't plunge the needle deeply into the pad, it wastes energy and can make your project stick to the pad more than necessary.

Weight Conversions

Ounces / Pounds	Grams	Ounces / Pounds	Grams
1oz	28g	16oz = 1lb	454g
2oz	57g	1.5lb	680g
3oz	85g	2lb	907g
4oz = 0.25 lb	113g	2.5lb	1134g
5oz	142g	3lb	1361g
6oz	170g	3.5lb	1588g
7oz	198g	4lb	1814g
8oz = 0.5lb	227g	4.5lb	2041g
9oz	255g	5lb	2268g
10oz	283g		
11oz	312g	Wool weights given in the	
12oz - 0.75lb	340g	materials section are approximate.	
13oz	369g	You may need a bit more or less	
14oz	397g	depending the size of your piece.	
15oz	425g		

Megan Nedds

If there was an award for "most-productive-needle-felter", Megan would surely win it! This Ohio based artist produces, on average, an astounding one commissioned piece per week. She is a sought after artist that combines the rare talents of intricate realism with efficiency.

Megan's work is breathtaking. Her brilliant ability to weave together the elements of beauty, realism, character and expression along with perfect proportions is stunning. She has developed original techniques for creating bird feathers and people often believe her needle felted birds are real at first glance. She's an expert armature maker and sculptor (polymer clay). She sculpts beaks, claws and noses for her creatures with great accuracy.

Armed with an art degree and a talent for business, Megan is serious about her profession. Felting since 2012, she regularly puts in over 40 hours a week and shows a stamina for felting that few can match. Megan sells her work and gets commissions through her Facebook page and Etsy accounts. She puts on seasonal workshops and sells kits and tutorials as well.

Advice: Most people are surprised at the time commitment to felting a piece and getting it firm and smooth. Take time to refine your piece.
Really study your subject matter and research it, see it from as many angles as possible before you start.

Business Advice: Try to build your social media following right away to connect with buyers. If you are selling on Etsy you must have patience. Sometimes it takes a few months to start selling.

On Facebook, Instagram and Etsy as:
@the woolen wagon

Favorite wool:
Local farms for Hampshire suffolk

Living Felt for MC1 batts

Suri alpaca for top coats

Basic Starter Kit

-Build Your Own-

1- Surface to felt on
1- Batt core (natural) 2 oz. or more
3- Batt colors 1 oz. each (your choice)
2- Combed top 1 oz. each (tan and black)
3- Six needles
1- Needle-holder tool

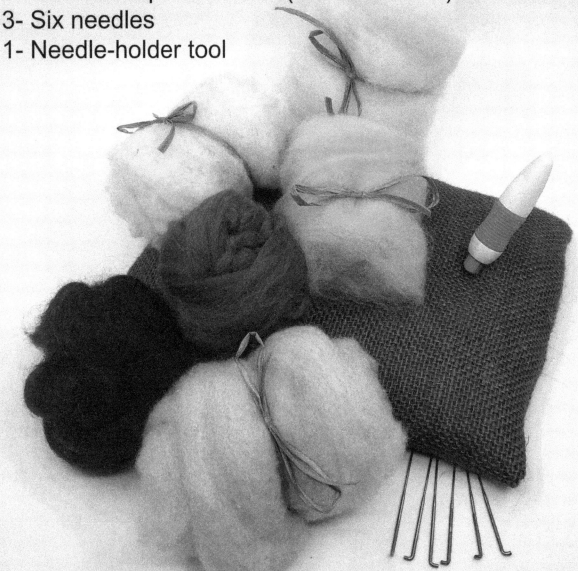

This kit is a picture of the minimum amount to get started in needle felting and not meant to be a representation of what is required for all the projects in this book. Each project lists amounts and colors necessary.

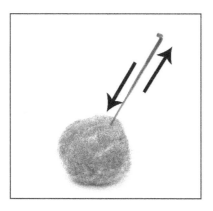

Using a needle - In needle felting, the needle is poked into the fiber and then removed at the same angle in which it was put into the wool. You can put a needle in at any angle, but you must remember to remove it at the same angle and not twist or bend it as it comes out or it could break the needle. The trick to remember is never to bend your needle while stabbing. If you are making a base or core, you will want to poke the needle in deeply. If you are adding surface color to the top, your needle should only penetrate the top 1/4". In needle felting, the act of using your needle is called "stabbing" or "needling".

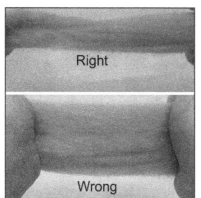

Dividing wool for use - When using batt, simply grab a hunk of wool and rip off the amount you need. For roving or top (pictured), measure out what you need and grasp in-between the area you want to break off. Pull with equal pressure and it should pull apart easily. If your hands are too close together it may not pull apart. You can also cut wool with scissors but this is not recommended.

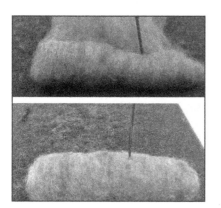

Making a cylinder core - Start by tightly rolling your wool and felt along the edge as you go. After you have rolled it tightly and to the proper size, stab down the edges and finish felting. Stabbing as you roll makes your core firm up more quickly.

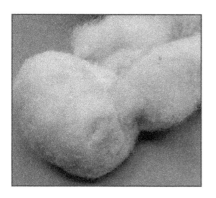

How to build round core/base - Start by tightly rolling your desired shape. Felt with each turn and roll. This gives you a firmer core faster than trying to felt a huge blob of wool all at once. The more "air" (or loft) you press out before you start to use your needle, the faster your felting time. Tuck in the outer edges of the roll and felt so that your shape begins to look rounded. Continue rolling, felting, tucking and turning until you reach the desired size.

Firmness levels - Needle felting sculpture falls into 3 categories of firmness: soft, medium and firm. A soft piece would be very squishy to the touch and would easily pull apart. Medium has some give to the thumb when pressed (pumpkin on right) and firm makes only a slight indentation when pressed into by the thumb (pumpkin on left). Most needle felting falls into the medium or firm category but the firmness level of a piece is a personal preference. It takes a lot of stabbing to get a very firm piece that doesn't give into the touch.

Making a smooth finish - Much of the smoothness of the finished product depends on the wool you start with. Batt is a good choice as most of the fibers will lay down flat. Top can be made smooth as well. Use a #40 or #42 needle for smooth finishes. New felters often underestimate the amount of stabbing it takes to make a piece smooth. Depending on the piece and its dimensions, you can also iron it or steam it. Some use shavers or scissors to trim unwanted stray pieces.

How to attach pieces together - In its simplest form, attaching two pieces together is as easy as layering one piece on top of another and plunging the needle from one piece and into another.

If you are attaching something like an ear or limb to a core, you can add a new layer of wool on top of both pieces to help cement them together.

Color blending with brushes- Sometimes, the perfect color you need is not available so you will need to blend colors together to make your own. You can do this by hand but it takes more time. Hand carders are the ideal but they are expensive. Dog grooming brushes work like miniature carders and are much cheaper to buy. Pick up each color onto the brush and use the brushes in an opposing manner to transfer wool back and forth until you've achieved the desired blended look.

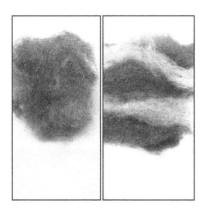

Color blending by hand - Layer the colors you wish to combine. Pull the entire piece in half with a ripping motion with your hands, then layer the bottom over the top and pull apart and layer again. Continue in this way until the colors have melded together.

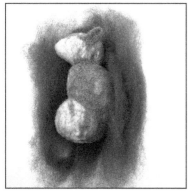

Adding a top coat - To add color to the top of your project, you can make a separate coat and then transfer it to your piece, or you can lay the colored wool directly onto the top of your natural colored core. The chipmunk project gives a good overview of top-coats.

Thin outlines - The best wool for making thin outlines is combed top. It is wispy and combed into long fibers making it perfect for outlining. You can break off very small strands and twist them between your fingers to make a clean line as you felt it onto your project.

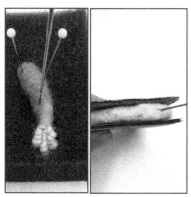

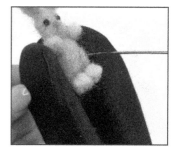

Making a small object - Small objects can be challenging. Usually it is best to hold down whatever you are making with sewing pins as you needle it. You can also put the object in between a piece of folded cardboard to use the cardboard as a holder so you don't poke your fingers.

Sarafina sells a leather tool that keeps your fingers safe while stabbing small items: The Stab and Grab Finger Protector.

Felted eyes - Creating realistic eyes with wool for both 2-D and 3-D projects takes skill (as evidenced in this portrait piece by Linda Wenger). If you choose to make your eyes through felting, study photographs of eyes and note the subtle shading and light spots that they have.
Photo: L.Wenger's Petable Portraits - Facebook

Pins or plastic bead eyes - Many people use these for animals that have dark eyes and large pupils. Their shiny appearance can look great in certain species. Make sure that when you add the eye, you've made an indent/socket and glue the eye in tightly. White, super and hot glue all work. Felt on eyelids to make them more realistic and perhaps a slight white dot painted onto the eye for more realism. Not suitable pieces that children will play with or have access to.

Glass or plastic eyes - These eyes are the most realistic and they come with clear or colored backgrounds. Glass eyes can be pricey. Many people make their own eyes by buying clear glass or plastic cabochons and either paint or use pre-made stickers to make the eye realistic. Etsy, Amazon and Ebay are sources.

Make your own eyes - You can model eyes from an oven-bake/polymer clay. Polymer clay comes in many colors and is easy to sculpt and harden in the oven. Follow package directions for baking. These eyes can be made flat or you can bake or glue them to the head of a pin to more easily insert them. Glaze the eye with clear nail polish or acrylic glaze for realism.

Projects

Using needle felting in your home decor is a fabulous way to display your work and creativity to the world. Even simple projects can make a big statement.

Cookie Cutter Ornaments

Holiday gift giving
and Christmas decor go
hand-in-hand with
Needle felting.

Felted pieces add a beautiful
touch seasonal wreaths

Cookie Cutter Heart

Materials needed:
Batt .5 oz, any color
Cookie cutter - heart or simple shape
Locks (natural or dyed)
Lace

Lesson 1: Practice proper needle techniques and learn how to felt firmly

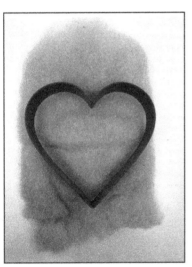

This simple cookie cutter heart is the best project to start with as a beginner. Practicing proper needle/stabbing technique to get the feel of pushing into and pulling out of the wool is important. This project is also necessary for beginners as it gives you an understanding of how long it takes to felt something firmly and the time it takes to give it a smooth finish. This heart will be felted to a solid-firm feel.

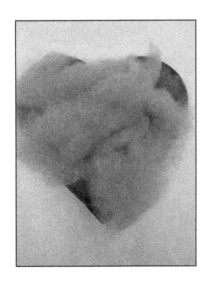

Start by pulling apart and putting down the first layer of the wool batt. Push the batt down firmly into the cutter. It will keep trying to poof out of the cutter but continue stabbing until it starts to flatten out. Start by stabbing into the middle of the heart and then work around to the edges.

Tip: When using a cookie cutter, be careful not to hit the needle against the metal as it will break easily.

After this first layer is felted down, the depth of the cutter should be about 1/3 full. Put down another layer of wool and felt it firmly (2 or 3 total layers). Your cookie cutter should be 3/4 full (approximately) by the time you are done.

Take the felted piece out of the cutter, flip it over and then felt down the underside. It will be fuzzy so smooth it out by continuing to stab. At this point you don't want to push the needle all the way through into the foam pad, keep your needle thrusts close to the top half of the heart. Short, even jabs will help smooth the finish.

After you have the desired smoothness, take it out of the cutter and go around the edges of the heart with your needle. You will be smoothing out edges and flattening the fuzz. If your heart developed any kind of asymmetrical issues you can correct this now.

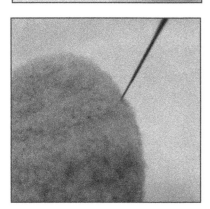

To finish the heart, use a fine needle, #40 or #42, to smooth it out. I use a multi tool for this that holds several #42 needles. Don't plunge the needle in too deeply, you don't want to go through to the other side at this point.

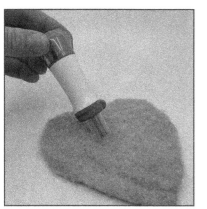

After you finish, you can leave it as it is or you can embellish it with natural color locks and lace. The lace is laid across the piece and gently felted with the locks on top to hold into place. To add the locks, simply arrange as you like and then gently felt down. Don't over-felt the locks or you will lose the curl.

At first glance this lesson may seem too basic and you may be tempted to skip it. However, this is an incredibly important exercise in understanding how long it takes to felt something firmly. I suggest you make this heart firm to the point that it feels very solid to the touch. This is a valuable lesson for future, more complicated projects.

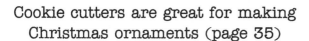

Cookie cutters are great for making Christmas ornaments (page 35)

Pillow with a heart of locks

Mikaela Bartlett

Mikaela is a Yorkshire, England based artist, famous for pieces that capture movement and expression. Conversing with Mikaela about her work was so enjoyable as she has a unique and refreshing perspective on felting and sculpting animals. There are few that can equal her talent in bringing the dynamic energy from the animal kingdom into wool sculpture. She infuses personality into her animals which allows you to see the world from their eyes.

Mikaela is faithful to the character of her subjects and she passionately studies them before beginning any piece. She collects photographs of her subjects from every angle in their natural environment. Mikaela believes you need to immerse yourself into their world in order to truly sculpt them well. Her work is incredibly realistic with superb attention to detail. She uses only wool, no glass eyes or clay details in her sculptures. Mikaela is a minimalist when it comes to sculpting. She works with only one type of needle, hand blends her own colors and uses few tools.

Mikaela began needle felting in 2016, having formerly been a ceramics artist. She has a large following on Instagram from which she sells most of her work.

Advice: Immerse yourself in the animal and his world. Collect photographs, put them in folders and refer to them often. You want to see pictures of them from every angle while you are working. Try to imagine movement in your animals. Think about giving them expression while you are making them.

Business: Get on Instagram, it's an artistic community. Interact with and encourage others and your following will grow.

Favorite wool: World of wool and Heidi Feather for needles.

Instagram: @mikaelabartlettfelt

39

Dryer Balls

Materials:
Batt: 1 oz. (each ball)
Combed top or batt: variety of colors
Pantyhose, string
Optional: Multi needle tool

Lesson 2: Making a round, 3-D ball

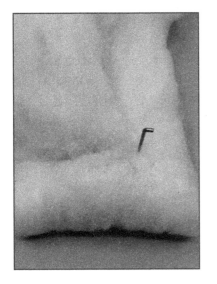

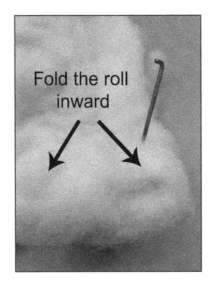
Fold the roll inward

Begin to roll a 7" piece (approx.) of the core batt as tightly as you can and felt down as you roll. It will start out looking like a cylinder. Rolling tightly saves extra felting work, you want to have as little "air" or loft in your ball as possible.

After each roll, turn the edges of the roll inward and felt down. So, roll..felt...turn edges in and felt...then roll and felt until you have a ball shape.

Keep turning your ball over and around, aiming for a circular shape. TIP: Using a 4 or more multi-needle holder tool will cut your felting time by 50%.

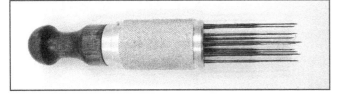

This 16 needle holder tool is the bad-boy I pick up when I need to get some felting done fast. Multi-needle tools are fabulous but make no mistake, this tool takes concentration to use and there will be blood if you try and watch TV while using it!

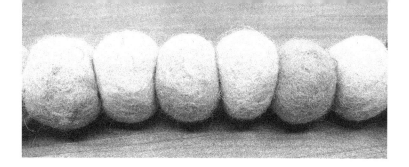

How do Dryer Balls work?

These wool balls absorb moisture from clothing in the dryer and allow for a more humid environment which in turn helps to reduce static cling. Dryer balls also cut drying time by fluffing clothes as they are tumbled. 3 - 6 in the dryer is ideal.

Alternative cores for Dryer Balls

The middle or core of a dryer ball can be made out of other materials. Some people cut up old wool sweaters and roll into a ball. Others recycle wool yarn and wind into a core. You can also take all the scraps from leftover wool and mix together for a more economical use of the core material. Just cover it all with batt or roving in your color choice.

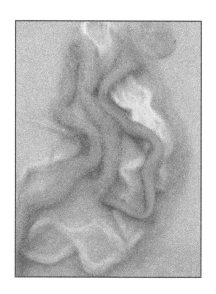

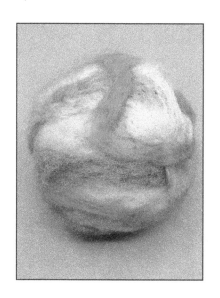

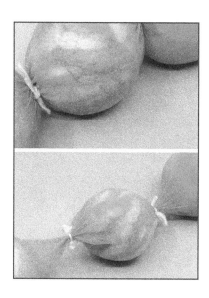

If you choose a multi color look, lay out your colors in a random pattern. This is a great place to use your colorful top or roving. You can also make a solid color ball, just make sure your top coat is thick enough or white will show through.

Roll the ball over the colors, tuck in edges and lightly felt down. Don't worry about felting down too firmly as this top coat will adhere during the next step of washing.

Wrap the balls in pantyhose and secure in-between each ball with string. You can put several balls in at once. Wash in your machine in hot water with your regular load (be mindful of color mixing when washing). These balls should go through the wash and dryer 2 or 3 times. Dryer balls will shrink in the dryer. Before and after picture shown.

Dryer sheets can contain a potentially harmful chemical called quaternary ammonium compounds (QACS) which have been known to cause and/or worsen asthma and skin irritations. QACS have also been linked to more serious long-term conditions like cancer and reproductive issues.

Autumn Pumpkin

Materials:

Batt: 1 oz. of core wool

Batt: dark and light orange (or use combed top)

Batt: olive or dk. green

1 Chenille stem

1 #20 green wire

Lesson 3: Learn how to sculpt a 3-D object

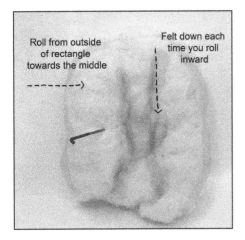

Roll from outside of rectangle towards the middle

Felt down each time you roll inward

Turn an 8" wide by 6" long rectangle of core wool inward from the sides, folding and rolling towards the middle and felting as you go.

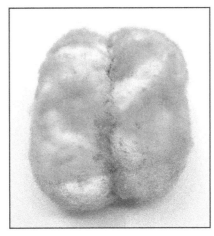

Felt down the middle and tuck in the sides.

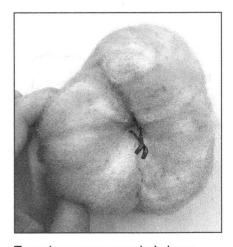

To make a more rounded shape, pinch the sides and felt as you are pinching. Felt an indented hole into the middle of the pumpkin.

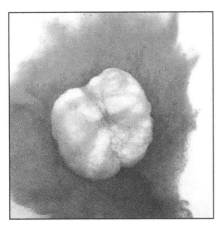

Place the pumpkin into the middle of your orange top coat.

Striated wool (wool with several color variations in it) is also a great choice for a top coat. Real pumpkins often have several layers of color and using multi-colored wool in this project lends the pumpkins a more realistic look. If you can't find striated wool for purchase, you can make your own by hand blending (see color blending under Basic Techniques).

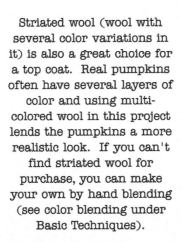

42

The top coat will make wrinkles as you fold it towards the top of the pumpkin and felt it down. These natural folds will mimic the growth lines on real pumpkins. Follow the lines with your needle to hold the folds in place.

 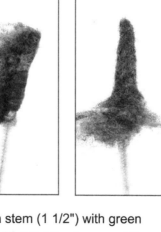

Wrap a stem (1 1/2") with green batt and felt tightly. Leave a bit at the end for attachment to the pumpkin. Attach the stem by making a small circle at the bottom end of the stem. Place into the round hole you indented in the middle of the pumpkin and felt over that with some extra green to attach.

Make the leaves by making a loose heart shape, felt flat and make indentations along the edges for realism.

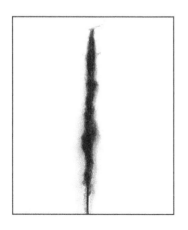

Tightly wrap a #20 piece of wire with green batt for curly tendrils. Wrap the tendril around a pencil to create a curled look then felt this curly piece to the middle, near the pumpkin stem.

Felt the leaf down in the middle and then smooth your pumpkin with a #40 needle.

Pumpkin Experiment
I gave this pumpkin a striated top coat (hand blended) and then I needle felted it. After he was completely needle felted and firm I put him in panty hose and processed him like a dryer ball before I added the stem. It made a more smooth top and it firmed up the core.

Make a pumpkin taller or more round simply by adding more wool to the beginning rolls or by wrapping additional batt onto the basic shape.

2-D Felted Rabbit

Materials:
Batt: .5 oz. tan or light brown
Batt; (small amounts) of pink, white, black
Top: black (small amount)
Pattern, page 99

Lesson 4: Sculpting a flat piece with multiple shapes and attachment of individual pieces

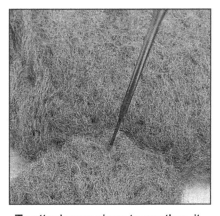

Cut out the rabbit silhouette in the back of this book or go online and search images for rabbit silhouettes, print and cut.

Using the silhouette as a guide, start to shape the basic parts of the rabbit. As you are shaping, lightly felt the pieces individually but do not attach them yet. As you are felting, keep checking the size of the parts you are making against the paper silhouette.

To attach one piece to another, it is ideal to have a slight bit of wool overage to lay on the other piece. If you don't have any wool overage, you can simply push one piece up to the other and overlap it and poke the needle through one part and into the other. The needle must go completely through each part. This will grab the fibers and begin to weave them together. You can also use a bit of extra wool, that is laid on top of both pieces and felted, to help fasten them together.

Take the body and the head and begin to felt them together by slightly overlapping the parts and stabbing at the seam. Continue felting along the seam until the two pieces are firmly attached. Keep checking your work by holding the body up to the paper silhouette and aim to keep it at the approximate size.

Continue adding body parts by attaching at the seams. If the pieces aren't overlapping well, use a bit of extra wool to overlay on the top (between the two parts) and it will give you that extra bit of fluff you need to more easily attach the pieces together. Continue to needle the body until it becomes firm and all pieces are securely attached

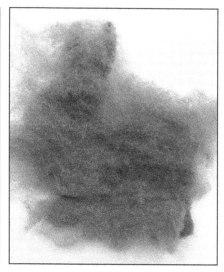

To cover the seams and give a fluffy appearance, you will need to add a top coat. Fluff out some batt and lay it on top of your piece then begin to tuck it in around the edges, felting as you go. Do not felt this coat down to tightly as you want to have a soft look with the top coat.

This is what the rabbit looks like after the top coat is added.

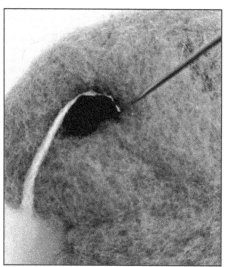

The first layer of the eye is a black almond shaped piece, felt directly onto the face. Add a thin rope of white to outline the black area.

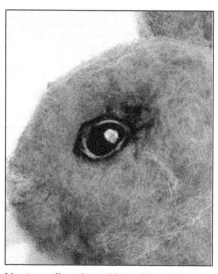

Next, outline the white with a thin rope of black and add a spot of white to the pupil. You can also fan out some very light, black eyelashes at the outer edge of the eye.

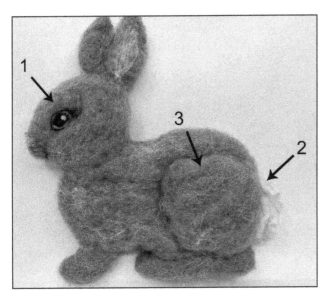

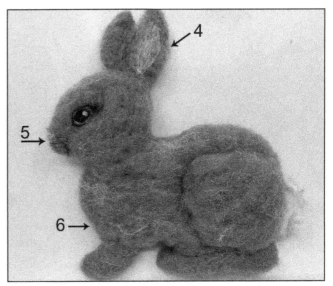

1. Finish details around the eye and then add your core color batt to fluff up any flattened down areas at the face.

2. For the tail, use curly wool locks or a bit of white to shape a circle and attach to his rear end.

3. Make a circle of wool for the thigh and gently felt down around the edges to attach.

4. Use a tiny puff of pink for the inner ear. Go for a transparent look don't make the pink too thick.

5. Add a triangular bit of pink for the nose, define the cheeks and add bits of batt to puff out as needed.

6. Using very thin wisps of white, lay around the body and head to make a more realistic top coat.

Upgrade your Rabbit

To make this curly/rex rabbit (which is closer to a 3-dimensional sculpture): make the head more full and rounded, position the ears so they are not flat against the head and add curly locks to the body. I have also used angora rabbit fur (as a top coat) to make an adorable bunny. Experiment with different colors to make a variety of rabbits. Rabbits like these take about 30 minutes and I make a few at a time to have on hand as I use them in all kinds of decor and gifts.

3-D Needle Felted Owl

Materials

Batt: .5 oz. dark brown or gray
Batt: white, tan, orange, black, golden yellow (small amounts)
Chenille stem (1)

Lesson 5: 3-D standing sculpture and beginning armature construction

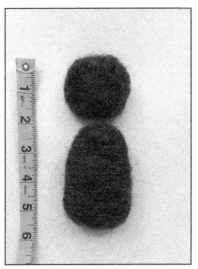

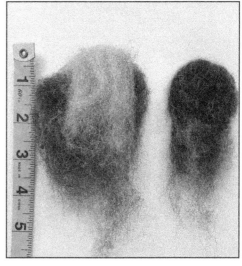

Form an oval for the **body** (5 1/2" long) and a circle (1 1/2") for the head. Do not felt flat. This owl has about a 1" thick puffy body.

Attach the **head** to the body and felt firmly.

Form the **wings** by taking a 4" piece of the body batt and folding it over in the middle. Add some white for shading and then felt the upper wing into a circular piece. Leave the bottom half wispy for the look of feathers. Attach the wings to the side of the body while felting down along the outer edges.

Should wool sculptures be firm or soft?

Every needle felter eventually develops their own style. Some felters prefer a bit of softness to their pieces and they feel felting a bit on the loose or soft side is more realistic. Others believe that felting firmly is best because firm pieces hold together better and they can add finer detail to them. Neither is right or wrong, it's just a matter of personal preference and artistic style.

Add a thin layer of white for the **chest area** and felt down lightly. Carry the white up into the face area as shown. Make white circles where you will place the eyes and leave the top area loose and feathery.

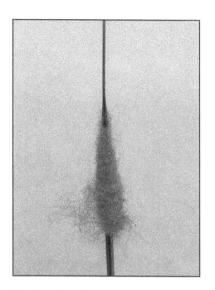

For the **beak**, wrap some orange wool around a needle, leaving a bit at the end loose. Slide this off your needle and carefully felt it directly onto the face. You will need to shape it by careful needling as you felt it. The loose, larger bottom edge goes against the face. Use a needle to pin the beak in place as you felt it down around it.

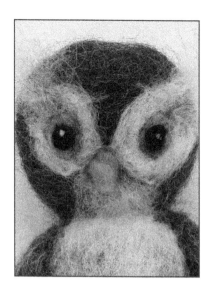

Add **eyes**. Use a golden yellow wool for the iris and black for the center. Add a small, round dot to the outer edge of the eyes for more realism. You can also use glass eyes (purchased online) and glue them on.

The **ears** are small pieces of body batt lightly folded over and felted down onto the head.

Finishing details include a black outline of the eyes and brown wool feather tufts on the outer top edge of the eyes. Add dark and tan feather spots to the body.

The **feet** are chenille stems bent into a cross shape, three of the claws will be extended forward and one extended towards the back (for standing stability). Twist/bend together as shown in the picture. The leg should be 1 1/2" long (for attachment purposes).

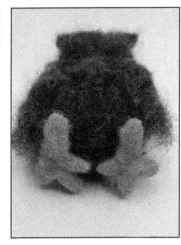

Wrap the toes in orange wool, pull tightly as you wind the wool around each area and then on up the leg. Felt carefully to keep it from unwinding.

Lay the feet on the back of the owl and position about 1" apart.

Place the body batt wool on top of the legs and felt all around the legs making sure the legs are secure.

Test the owls ability to stand and adjust the feet as needed.

Owl Decor

A group of owls is called a parliament

There are over 225 different species of owls

50

Woodland Chipmunk

Chipmunk

Materials
Batt: .5 oz. natural/core
Batt: reddish brown, tan, dark gray brown, white, pink
Top: white, black
Chenille stem
Pattern, page 99

Using your chipmunk pattern (pg. 99) begin to shape the body and head pieces separately, felting to a medium firmness.

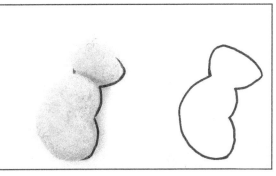

Check the shape of the body against your pattern as you attach the head to the body. It is very easy to get off track at this stage and you want to keep your proportions as close to realistic measurements as possible. Using a simple pattern is a time saving device as it will minimize sizing mistakes.

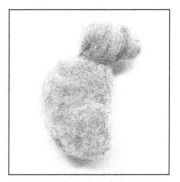

Attach the head and the body, make sure you double check the placement and proportions.

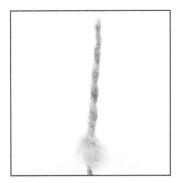

For the tail, tightly wrap 3" of a chenille stem with core wool. Felt carefully and leave a 1/2" piece of unfelted wool at the end (the edge where it will be inserted into the bottom).

Bend the bottom of the tail stem into a circle. Press that circle into the body, add wool and felt to the body. For the haunch/thigh, stab into the wool around the outlined area, this will make an indented area and the haunch will rise up as you felt around it. Add a bit of wool if it isn't full enough. 52

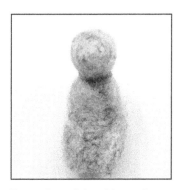

Front view of the chipmunk.

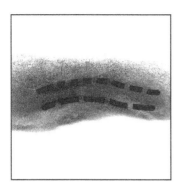

Make a top coat, or pelt, by layering three colors: tan, reddish brown and gray brown. Make the pelt the approximate size/length of the chipmunk, including the tail.

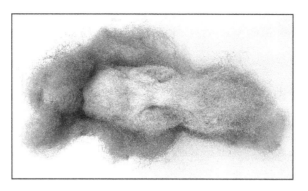

Before wrapping the pelt around the chipmunk, felt white onto his belly and up through his chin. Then lay the pelt over the back-top from the nose to the tail and wrap it around the entire body except for the white area. Felt down lightly with a fine gauge needle.

Felt tightly around the tail and the neck in a ring like pattern

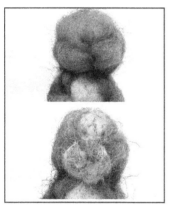

The top coat/pelt will end at the face. Gently tuck in around the face and felt down. Add white on the cheeks and chin and add a triangle of pink for the nose.

For the arms, take a small amount of pelt/top coat and roll into a cylinder. Add pink to the tip (for paws) and then felt down. Leave a small tuft at the end for attachment. Indent the top edge of the paw for digits.

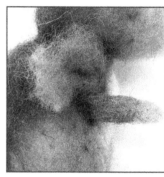

Attach the arm in the area shown and bend slightly at the elbow. Stab down the fluff at the end to blend in with the body and felt securely.

Why Use Patterns/Guides?

I make patterns for some sculptures because it's a disheartening experience to get halfway through your project and realize your proportions are off. To make patterns I search for an image from a book or online search, get measurements and then draw a simple outline from that. You only want a very basic proportional outline, do not attempt to make an exact copy of the image. You are aiming for good dimensions only. Skeletal drawings are also helpful in seeking out size guidance.

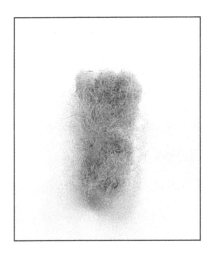

For the feet make a small, pink rectangle. Create three small toes at the top by felting downward. Attach the feet to the bottom of the body. Test him for standing power and balance.

Ears start off as small triangles in the pelt color with a bit of pink added to the middle. Felt down the triangle until you have softened the angles into curves as shown. Leave fluff at the bottom for attachment.

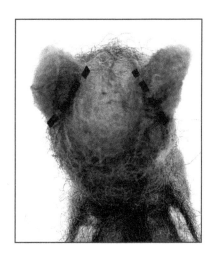

Ears are attached at an angle as shown in the photo. Refer to pictures of real chipmunks if you are having trouble. Ears can be tricky to place correctly. Make sure you do a very light initial felt down of them in case you have to reposition.

For the stripes use combed top in white and black. Starting at the shoulders, go downward and make a curve outward with the white. Outline the white with black and the middle of the back is a simple black stripe. Carry the black through to the tail.

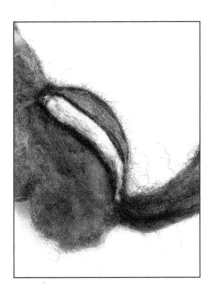

Don't felt the stripes down to firmly, you want to give them a soft look.
Note: Customize the stripes accordingly if you choose to make a chipmunk indigenous to your region. Stripes vary according to geographical location.

To finish the face you will want to continue to refine the head's oval shape. Stab indentations where the eyes will be placed and then add eyes by using felted balls, or glass eyes. Outline the eyes in white and needle the nose until it's proper chipmunk size.

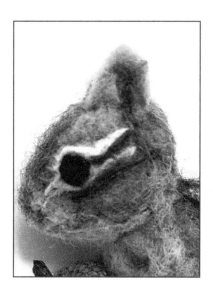

Add white and dark brown stripes to the side of the face.

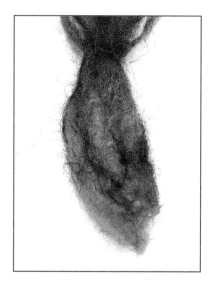

Keep the tail somewhat fluffy and add a shading of black on top of the tail.

Chippy Tips:

There are over 25 different species of chipmunks. Think about customizing your project to the type of species native to your area. Look up images of chipmunks for your locale: different colors, different stripes but they are all about the same size.

Project Planning

After you learn the fundamentals of needle felting you will naturally start to develop your own ideas for projects and designs. Spontaneous felting is great but a big or complicated project takes planning.
Outlining those projects out in advance will increase your chances of success.

Start a folder for ideas: drawings, pictures and wool samples. Use the Project Planning page (pg. 101) for help in organizing and coordinating your project.

Collect photographs - It helps to have reference photos from as many angles as possible when you are working. I put all my online photos in a Pinterest board or a folder on my computer.

Get a taxidermy catalog - There are many pictures of animal skeletons and muscle structure as well as mouth and beak close-ups. Catalog

Purchase materials in advance as much as possible. It's hard to get everything you need (at this time) from a one-stop shopping experience. I usually wind up on several websites as well as Etsy for more specialized items like glass eyes or exotic wool.

Follow your favorite felters on Instagram, Pinterest and various other social media sites for inspiration and new techniques.

Living Felt Store, Texas

Sheep Family

Free standing Sheep

Materials:
Batt: .5 oz natural color/core wool or gray batt
Batt or top: black, pink and brown
Locks: white or black (small size)
Black Sculpy/polymer clay for feet
Thin stick (skewer works well)
Eyes: black pins or glass eyes

Lesson 7: Make a free standing sheep without an armature. Your wool sculpting abilities will take a leap with this sheep but the step-by-step tutorial breaks it down into simple tasks.

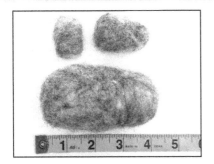

Make the body, neck and head with core wool. The body is a tightly rolled cylinder, the head is a cylinder with the back of the head being thicker (oval) and the neck is a simple rolled cylinder.

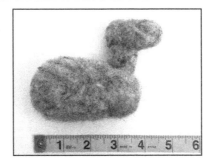

Attach the neck to the body and felt down firmly. Felt the head onto the neck.

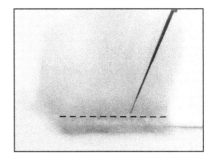

To make the legs, roll batt tightly on a thin stick and felt down along the edge with each turn. This gives you a firm leg for the sheep to stand on. Leave a little loose wool at the top.

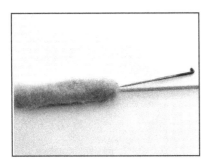

Stab the bottom hoof area to make a flat-foot surface for him to stand on. Carefully slide the leg off the stick and felt any lose areas.

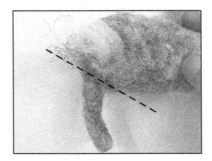

Attach the leg directly under the body using the loose wool to help anchor it . Felt it firmly to the body and then felt the loose wool down into the thigh area.

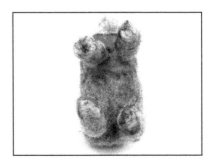

Leg placement is important, test as you felt and make sure your placement will help him to stand upright.

Test the sheep's legs to make sure they are felted firmly enough to hold him in a standing position.

Proportion

Are you struggling with getting the perfect proportions on your project? There are several things that can help. First, take a picture of your piece. The camera often reveals issues with a new eye. Also, check images online for different angles and new perspectives. Try walking away from it for a few days, this is often the biggest help. When you come back to it you can more easily see what's gone wonky and what needs to be corrected.

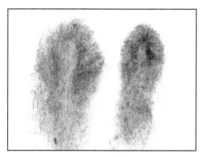

Ears -The piece on the left is how you will shape the ear before it is felted. Add a touch of pink or peach to the middle. Leave the bottom unfelted. The ear on the right is what it looks like after felting.

Attach the ears to the back of the head using the loose wool at the bottom of the ear. Shape the ears by carefully felting around the outside edges.

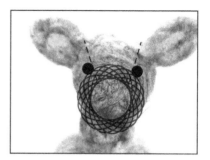

Needle (gently stab) along the dotted lines to help you create contours. Make indentations for eyes. Follow the spiral circle area to slim the muzzle.

Cover the sheep ears, face and legs with either black or white, according to the type of sheep you are making. Add the topcoat of locks to the body.

Add small amounts of wool to the circled areas shown. Felt down lightly. This creates and defines the cheek and chin area.

The red area (color emphasized) are thin lines of pink for the nose and the lips.

Side view of the face.
Note: For whatever breed you prefer to create, it's always good to go to online image sources for more details.

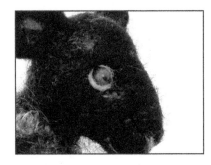

This sheep has eyes that are black pins that I carefully painted golden irises onto with acrylic paint. You can also felt an eye or use glass eyes. Add a thin line of white to outline.

Front view of the face. Add a smidgen of gray to the nose area to highlight it.

To make a white sheep, follow the same basic steps outlined in the black sheep but use white core wool and white locks.

The white sheep has black sewing pins as eyes with a thin piece of white roving carefully felted over the eye as an eyelid.

The details of the face for the white sheep are more delicate and her muzzle is slightly more tapered. The lips and nose are outlined in pink and black.

The coat of this sheep is small, white locks. You can also just use a flat batt for the wool coat as well. For this sheep the wool extends over her forehead.

Use an oven-bake polymer clay to make feet. Shape with your fingers and a small knife. Indent the back half of the hoof.

Make sure you test your feet before baking by holding them up to the legs to check size. Bake according to package directions. Glue on with hot glue or white glue after baking.

Baby Lamb

Materials:
Batt .30 oz. natural/core wool
Batt: pink, black
Locks: curly and white
Chenille stem
2 black pins for eyes

This lamb is about half the size of the adults with more diminutive and delicate features.

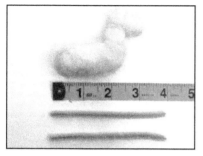

Make the body, neck and head as the adult sheep but smaller. I chose to use chenille stems for the legs for standing power. Very thin legs are hard to felt firmly unless they have the support of wire.

Felt the wool onto the chenille stems by wrapping the stems tightly and felting as you turn them. Put the legs on the body and bend at the points shown. Overlay additional wool and felt down to hold the legs to the body.

This is how your finished legs should look.

Make ears as you did for the adult sheep and felt on. Begin to refine the muzzle.

Felt down and indent/refine the muzzle along the dotted lines. Indent the eye area and glue in black pins or felt eyes. Add pink for the nose and black for lips.

Add the curly top coat and a tail. Lambs have longer tails than adults.

Selling your Work - Business Advice

The price tag is the first impression you get to make on a customer. It tells them it's quality and you're proud of what you made. Never undervalue that. M.C.

Pet commissions can be a full time income. You can have a great business doing pet portraits. A.M.

Don't worry about what anyone else is doing. If you are in love with your work then others will fall in love too. Someone might copy your idea, someone might felt better than you do, someone might have different prices, but only you can make what you make and are brave enough to share it. S.R.

Social media is a powerful advertising tool. It's helpful to join pages that have a connection to your art's theme. Members who are passionate about your subject matter will get the word out for you. L.W.

Don't undervalue your work to attract people. Extremely low prices may lead buyers to think it's of poor quality, not a collectible. Also, if you develop followers and your pieces suddenly shoot up to 4, 5 or 6 times you may lose them. Start pricing reasonably and increase your price as your skill increases. Take good pictures from all views and write descriptions as if there was no picture. Imagine describing your piece to someone who can't see, so that they can visualize the item...Have different price points and try to have a variety of items. Some whimsical, some natural, ornaments or hanging objects plus 3-D items. Or, if you work in larger pieces, make some smaller pieces to induce buyers who don't have as much display space-or money. H.L.

Instagram, at present, is the number one social media platform for artists to show their work and build a following. Many artists also have a thriving business selling from Instagram. L.R.

The laws about selling toys varies from country to country. Generally, it is recommended that felters do not sell their pieces as toys because toys must be rigorously tested before selling in the general market. Always include a tag on your items that declare that your felted work is not a toy and not intended for children. L.B.

If you are just starting out selling on Etsy, be patient. Sometimes it takes a couple months to make your first sale but if your work is good and prices are fair it will eventually snowball and orders will come in. R. K.

Know your target market. Yes, your items may take you many hours especially as you are beginning. Start with your labor cost and approximate materials cost. Increase your prices slightly with each new piece and improved technique. When you have reached your local market budget limit, start going online. If you are doing this as a new business have a range of prices of similar items as well as one of a kind pieces. Remember, you can always put items priced too high on sale but it is more difficult to put unsold/less refined items back in among your improved items and expect the same price point L.J.

When doing fairs, you need to have pieces at different price points (to attract all types of buyers) and business cards. A customer might buy a small piece but come back later for custom work. V.H.

Megan Nedds

62

Kiyoshi Mino

Kiyoshi Mino is a remarkable needle felter. Kind hearted and sincere, Kiyoshi has a passion for endangered species and has made a name for himself sculpting life sized, realistic animals. Constantly pushing the boundaries of needle felting, his creations are installed in museums and galleries worldwide.

His passion for needle felting began in 2011 with a desire to find an interesting new use for the wool from his farm. Kiyoshi is self taught with a natural talent for sculpting. After taking a simple introductory course for needle felting, Kiyoshi found himself in a world of new possibilities and his inventiveness with wool is now admired all over the world

Although Kiyoshi's animals are incredibly detailed and perfectly proportioned he admits he has a free spirited style and confesses that he rarely measures anything, preffering to eyeball his pieces and adjust as he works.

Kiyoshi works in needle felting full time, selling much of his work through galleries. He is a sought after teacher and his domestic and international workshops now fill much of his schedule.

Instagram: @kiyoshiminofelt

Advice: Use a light touch with the needle. Don't push it too deeply into the piece. Start out using less wool than you think you will need, projects often get too big and it's more difficult to take wool off than it is to add it on.
Favorite wool: Merino from Living Felt

Juvenile Orangutan

Needle Felted Orangutan

Materials:
Batt or roving: .5 oz. brown/tan
Batt: light peach, dark. brown, reddish brown, orange, black, white (small amounts)
3 Chenille stems

Lesson 8: Learn how to make a simple armature

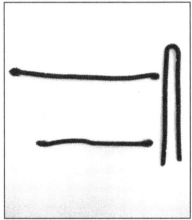

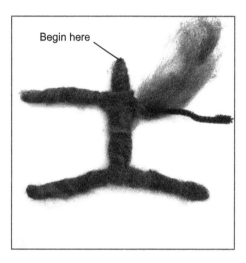

Begin here

The body is a full chenille stem bent in half, the arms are 8" and the legs are 6" long. Pinch the ends of the stems for the arms and legs over by 1/4" so the edges are not exposed metal.

Lay the body stem in the middle of the arm and legs as shown. Twist the arms and legs around the body and make sure the twist is secure and the arms and legs do not slide. Twist the bottom edge of the body upwards and wind around his bottom to secure.

Begin wrapping the armature with the core wool. Holding the wool at a slight angle start in the neck area and go down the middle. Follow outward at the legs - go down and back for each leg. Go up the middle again and then do each arm. Finish back in the middle and give him a full belly. Felt down as you do each part and then around the whole body when you are done to make sure your wrapping is secure.

Many needle felted armatures are made using plain wire. The reason chenille stems/pipe cleaners are used in this project as opposed to plain wire is because the wool tends to stick a bit better to the chenille when it's being wrapped, therefore it's easier for the beginner. However, if you want to use wire you certainly can, there will be no difference in the finished project.

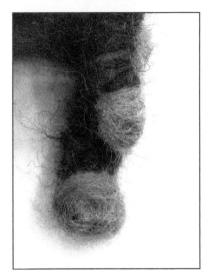

To make the face, use an oval ball of peach and felt onto the face. Make the eye areas as flat circles, out of peach, and felt flat to the head. Indent holes in the eye areas for eye sockets. Add black pupils and tiny white dots in the corners.

The mouth is a thin brown/black line. The nose is a very small bit of brown, it is flat and is more of a shadow to suggest the inner part of the nose.

For the ears, make ovals out of light peach and felt directly onto the head.

Wrap light peach to the feet and hands and felt down.

Orangutans are among the most intelligent primates on the planet. They can use tools, build elaborate nests and they have distinct social cultures. These majestic animals are a highly endangered species. This project depicts a juvenile Bornean orangutan.

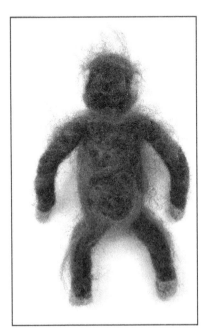

Add some orange to outer edges around the body to accentuate the fuzzy top fur. Pull it gently, after you've felted down to make it stand up.

His poseable body makes him the perfect laptop companion!

Steffi Stern is a passionate needle felting evangelist. She has an energy and zest for life that is contagious and I absolutely loved interviewing this UK based, needle felting expert. Steffi works to inspire people to live the creative life and to try their hand at becoming a "maker".

The Waldorf movement and its emphasis on sustainable/natural crafts motivated Steffi to start felting in 2002 with her children and now, more than a decade later, she is an accomplished needle felter, author and owner (along with her partner Sophie) of a thriving business called "The Makerss" which is both a physical shop as well as an online website.

A woman of stamina and zeal, Steffi and her partner teach an astounding number of local based workshops a year (over 100!) as well as hosting their own retreats and workshops through their business. She firmly believes that hands-on workshops are essential to an individuals growth in needle felting. She also enjoys hosting visitors in their shop and loves making a cup of tea for those who have traveled long to get there.

Favorite products: The wool and products sold by the Makerss. They are throughly field tested and approved.

www.themakerss.co.UK

Clare Lepetit is a friendly, kind-hearted encourager. A great conversationalist, you instantly feel at ease in her presence. She started felting in 2011 and was instrumental in popularizing the craft in Europe. Clare began felting in the UK but she now resides in France in a quaint village where she needle felts, raises her family and serves as an admin for the 20,000 member "Needle Felting" group on Facebook.

Clare's needle felting beginnings include several interesting ventures. Struggling to find suitable felting wool in the UK and France, she began importing wool from Germany which she then in turn sold to local felters. Clare also ran a successful business making beautiful felted angels which she shipped around the world. As a needle felting trailblazer in the EU, she was asked to test and then sell the Addiquick needle felting machine, the first electric needle felting machine in the world.

Favorite wool: German Mountain wool as a core wool. Russian Karacul for cores that need to be very solid. Merino batting and tops for surface work, hair and fluff. **Supplier**: Wollknoll-Germany
Favorite tools: The AddiQuick (Selter), Zulli-tool from Sarafina

"Needle Felting" Group - Facebook

Needle Felted Dog Mini-poodle

Materials:
Batt or Roving: .30 oz. gray
Locks: gray (for the top coat)
Top: black
2 black pins
1 chenille stem

Lesson 9: Make a standing armature with balance and symmetry

Cut a chenille stem in half, then bend as shown. Pinch and fold the ends of the stems at the bottom.

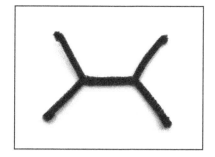

Place the two backs on top of each other and twist where the legs meet.

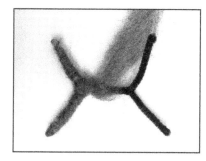

Begin wrapping the legs. Wrap through the middle and then to the other legs on the opposite side.

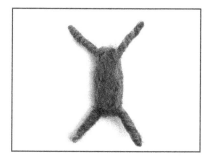

Make the middle area thicker by adding more roving. Felt down as you go.

Bend the legs to the proper shape and test the ability of the dog to stand.

Add a small, loose roll for the neck and felt at the base, leaving the upper neck loose.

Shape the head and muzzle by making an oval for the main part of the head and a smaller, oblong piece for the nose/muzzle. Felt on the muzzle.

Sideways view of muzzle/head.

Attach the head to the loose area of the top of the neck and felt head securely. Add a tail (no stem/wire in tail) by making a roll on a stick, felting it down and felting the loose area to the bum.

Begin adding the top coat. For this poodle I'm using blue face leichester wool locks in gray with natural crimp to it. You can use any crimped wool or simply a smooth wool depending on the breed you make.

Make indentations for the eyes and place in the eyes of choice with glue. I've used pins here. Make a black nose and outline the lips in black. Give the cheeks tufts of wool to fill out the muzzle.

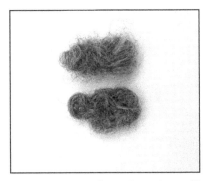

Make two ears from the crimped/curled wool

Place the ears and felt on securely.

Side view of finished dog.

The great thing about an armature is the animals ability to be posed. Here is his sitting pose.

Inspiring Artists

Dayna McFadden - Needle felt artist
@MyHeartFeltFriend

Cindy-Lou Thompson - @chicktincreations
Award-winning dogs

Linda Wenger - L.Wenger's Petable
Portraits on Facebook

Mouse

Standing Mouse Armature

Materials:
Batt or Roving : .5 oz in white or tan
Batt: white or brown for top coat
Batt or Top: Flesh color or pink
Top: black, dark brown
Scarf - color your choice in batt or top
22 inches wire

Lesson 10: Intermediate armatures

TIP: Roving is easier to use than batt when wrapping armatures because it is sold in rope form. Batt must be torn into strips before using.

Learning how to do armatures well brings your felting up to a new level . Be patient and felt carefully. Wire can and does break needles when you stab it accidentally.

I used string coated wire with this project as it is easier to twist and wrap roving on. You can also use plain wire as well.

Alternatively, You can use pipe cleaners for this project but they aren't quite as strong as wire.

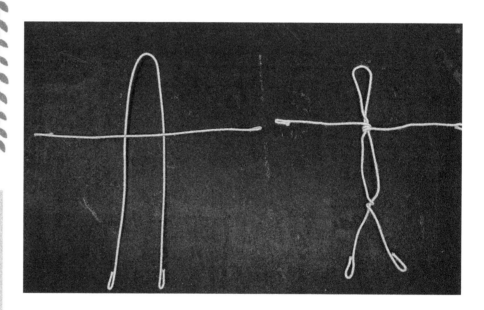

Measure wire for the body: 13". For the arms: 4 1/2". The tail: 5 1/2"

Pinch the wire at each end for feet and hands. This keeps sharp wire from poking through your project.

Fold the body wire in half as shown and place the arms across the breast.

Pinch the neck area together then twist the arms around the neck.

At the crotch area, twist the wire together.

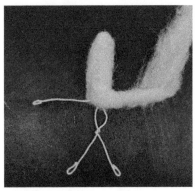

Starting at the top of the head, wrap the roving in a downward motion, making sure to pull it as tightly as possible as you are wrapping. Felt down at the end of each limb before moving to the next limb.

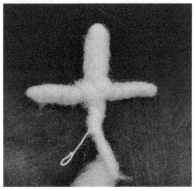

Continue wrapping to the other arm and then down to the stomach area. Go down each leg and back up again.

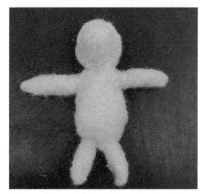

Wrap the middle area so that he has a chubby tummy. Bend the head forward at the halfway mark. This then becomes the muzzle. Wrap the muzzle until it blends with the neck.

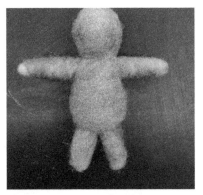

Make a top coat of white or brown/tan and felt down.

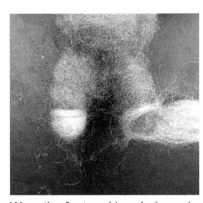

Wrap the feet and hands (paws) with the pink/flesh color wool. Felt down tightly.

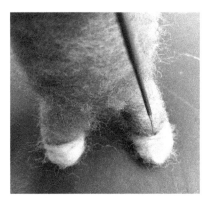

Push the mouse down onto your felting surface so that his heels press the front of the feet forward. In this crease, felt down across the middle. This gives him a flat foot to stand on.

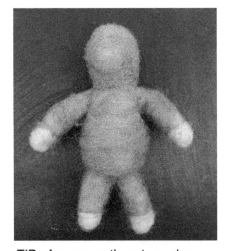

TIP: As you continue to work on and refine various parts of your mouse, you may need to add more top coat if the white starts to show through.

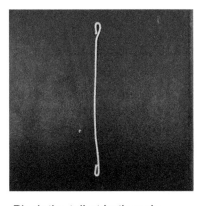

Pinch the tail at both ends.

Wrap the tail tightly with peach. Felt carefully along the wire holding your needle at an angle. This keeps it from unraveling. Leave one end unfelted.

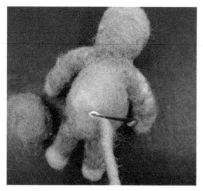

Attach the tail by bending the circular part of the wire and placing in his bum area. Use a bit of top coat to place on top of the wire and carefully felt all around to attach the tail firmly.

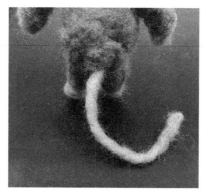

The tail holds the mouse up to a standing position, make sure it is felted securely.

Refine the muzzle to a more tapered profile. Make indents for eyes.

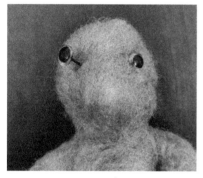

For wired glass eyes, place a tiny bit of white glue in the eye indents and then poke the wire for the eyes into the holes. You can also use felted balls or pins.

Make a nose with the wool used for the tail and paws. Outline with a thin line of a matching, darker brown.

Ears are the top coat wool that are twisted in a spiral shape and then felted down. Add flesh colored wool to the middle. Felt down around the circle of pink/peach. Leave wool at the bottom.

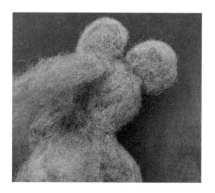

Using the bottom part of the unfelted wool, place the ear onto the back of the head and blend the unfelted wool onto the head by felting.

The mouth is a thin black line felted from the nose to slightly under the chin as shown.

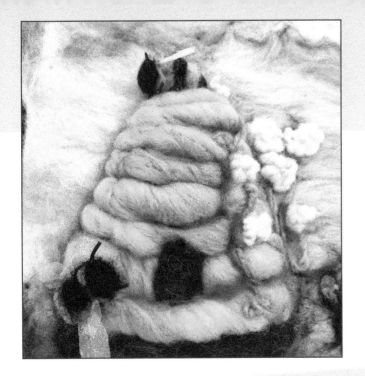

2-D Needle felted Landscape

Materials:

Wool fabric (or any dense weave fabric for backing)
11 x 14 (with overage for framing if desired)
Combed top: .33 oz. yellow
Combed top (small amounts): white, light blue, dark blue, dark brown, tan, light green, dark green, white, golden yellow, black, light purple, dark purple, light red, dark red
#22 wire (for bee legs)
White ribbon (translucent) for wings

Lesson 11 - This 2-dimensional landscape is a needle felted piece created with the flowing fibers of combed top, which is the secret to its brush-stroke/painted look. Use your creativity to change the colors or add more flowers.

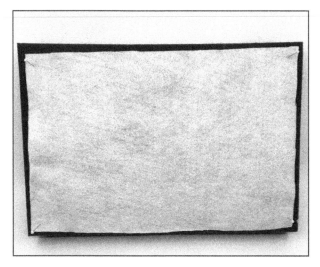

The background can be almost any type of fabric or pre-felted wool or felt (I have used 100% wool fabric here). It should have some thickness to it. Stretch out the fabric onto a piece of foam that matches the size of your picture and remove the wrinkles but do not overstretch. Pin the four corners with sewing pins.

Begin by layering on the sky and the clouds with blues and whites. For this type of picture it's best to keep all the fibers going in one direction for the background. Layer on the ground and grass with the greens and browns. It's preferable to have varying shades of color to give your picture depth.

Next, felt down all the layers and add more top as needed to cover empty spaces. This entire piece is loosely needle felted to keep a soft, wispy look.

Begin to add shading. Small wisps of gray, tan and yellow for the clouds. Dark blue and gray for the sky. Refer to the finished picture for shading placement.

What's the difference between a needle felted picture and a wool painting?

Needle Felted Picture - Any 2-D work of art using wool as its medium and is needle felted.

Wool Painting - This term can have two meanings. It can be used to describe a needle felted picture (above) or some artists use this term to describe a picture that is made with combed top, layered on a base and framed under glass, never having been needle felted.

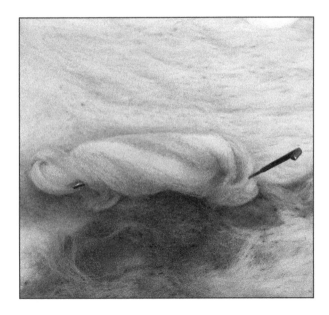

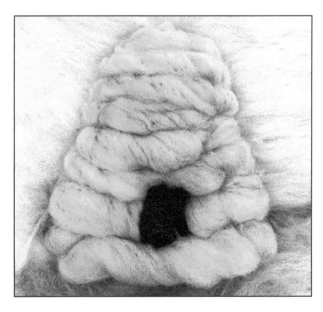

To start the hive, work from the bottom up. Twist together yellow and tan top and fold the ends of the twist under itself at the edges and felt down. Continue adding twists and building each layer upwards.

As each layer is finished, felt between the twists but don't felt this hive flat, you want a slightly raised piece. Add a door with dark brown. For shading add some tan in-between some of the twists.

To make the bottom board of the skep/hive, felt down a brown layer underneath of the hive and extend slightly out beyond the width of the bottom.

To make the daisies, start with a twist of white and felt it into a figure 8 directly onto the picture.

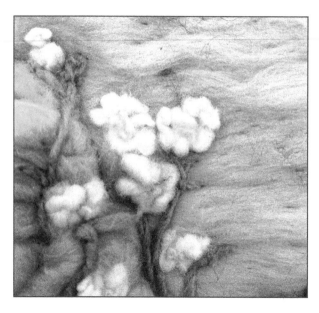

Continue twisting, layering and felting down untill you have a full looking flower. Make an uneven number of flowers.

Add the yellow centers. For the stems and leaves, twist a light green piece of top and felt it down onto the picture as you place it.

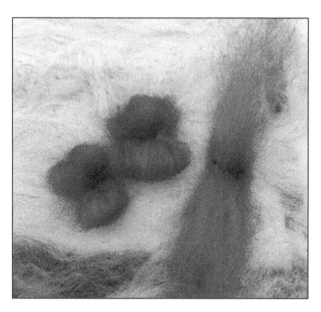

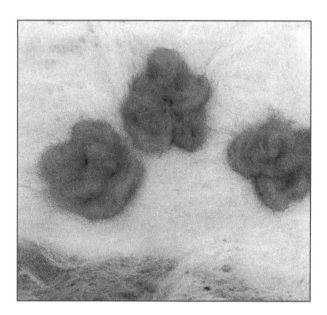

The poppies start out by laying down a piece of red, felting the middle down then folding each part towards the middle and felting where it meets.

Do this process twice more to make more petals. Do not felt completely flat, leave slight puffs in the edges. Felt down where the petals would naturally meet the middle of the flower.

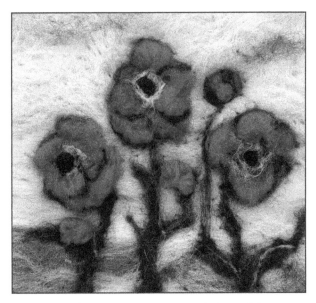

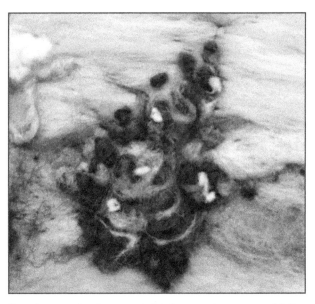

Give each flower center a white circle and then put a black circle/ball in the middle of that. Outline in a blue or purple with thin, twisted strands. Make the stems and leaves in dark green by twisting the wool and felting down the strands.

For the purple flowers, twist for petals as you did the daisies but use multi colored strands of purple. Add white accents after the purple petals are in place. Use dark green to add stems and leaves.

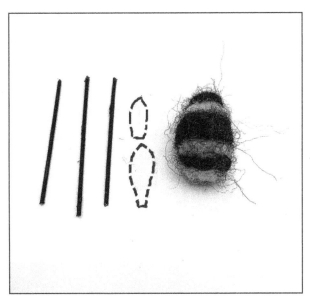

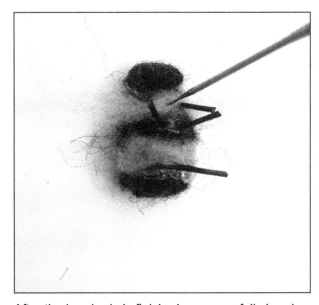

Make the core body of the bee in black or yellow by felting an oval out of batt. Add contrasting stripes and give him a white bum. For the head, add an oval black piece to the top of the body. The legs are made of florists wire #22 and painted black. The wings are cut from a white, translucent, ribbon. 2 wings per side, one wing being slight larger than the other. Cut out 4 wings total, for each bee.

After the bee body is finished, very carefully bend the legs in half and use the tiniest dot of hot glue (or glue type of your choice) to secure to the body. Use corresponding colored wool to lay over the glue area and felt carefully down to cover the glue spots.

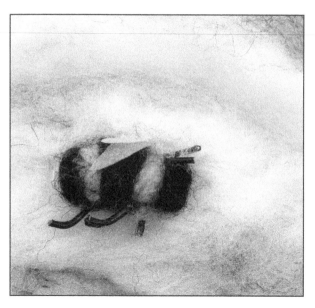

Add the wings by careful gluing. The larger wing on the bottom, the smaller wing on the top.

For the flying bee, his legs are bent backwards to simulate movement. Felt him directly onto the cloud.

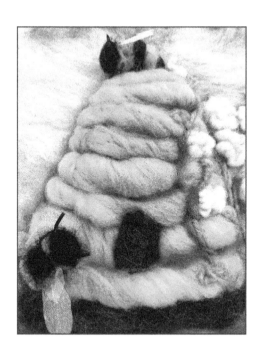

You can either felt down or glue your bees to the skep/hive.

Tip: After you finish your picture the fabric will be quite felted to your under-pad. Carefully peel off the fabric by firmly grasping the top two corners and slowly pulling with equal pressure on both hands.

2-D Needle felted Bumblebee

Materials:

Fabric background - wool fabric (best) or cotton, 8 x 10

Batt: (small amounts) black, white, yellow, tan, gray, orange

Pattern, page 98

pins, pencil

Lesson 12: This flat, 2-D bumblebee is created completely with batt. Batt is a great fiber for most 2-D pictures as it blends very well and can give your picture almost a photographic look.

Higher gauge (finer) needles work best for 2-D pictures on fabric (unless the fabric is very stiff). A multi-tool with 5, #40 needles are perfect for this application.

Making 2-D projects on fabric backgrounds is enjoyable because these projects can be used for all kinds of home decor.

Framing is one option but consider pillows, wall-hangings and table runners. Needle felting on clothing is beautiful as well.

Get your felted projects out into the world in practical ways so they can be appreciated in everyday settings.

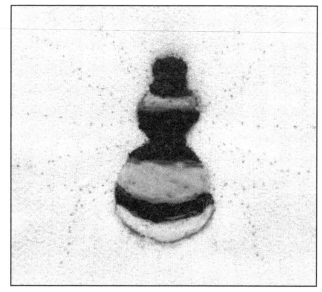

Pin the pattern (page 98) onto the fabric. Then, using a sharp pencil or a thick needle, go around the entire image poking a hole through the paper and onto the fabric (do this very lightly). Remove the paper and use the holes as your guide to felting.

Begin with the body. Felt down the black, yellow and white. Use the tan for shading along the edges of yellow and black. Outline his bumblebee bum with a thick strand of tan. The head is black with a shade of tan and his eyes are black balls.

Begin the wings with a layer of white. Shade lightly with gray and then add the black lines for wing veins. Add small white dots to the eyes.

Outline the antenna and the legs with black. Shade the bottom legs slightly with gray. Use smidges of yellow for highlights on the wings and burnt orange as shading along the black stripes

To make any felted 2-D piece into a pillow, search online for sewing instructions

Dani Ives

www.daniives.com
Instagram: @begoodnatured

Dani Ives is a talented and accomplished needle felter who specializes in 2-Dimensional, wool paintings that are needle felted. Articulate and friendly, she's a former zoo educator with a masters in conservation ecology who has turned her passion for animals and flora into a beautiful art form.

Needle felting since 2011, Dani has developed new techniques for 2-D wool painting and has become foremost in her field. Her expertise in blending fiber and color gives her wool paintings amazing realism. At first glance, many people are surprised that her pieces are made out of fiber and not paint. Dani's portraits are true to life in a way that captures not only precise anatomical realism but expression and personality as well.

A capable business woman, Dani has one of the largest social media followings of any needle felt artist as a result of being featured in several online news outlets in the early days of social media. This popularity has translated into a thriving business of sales and commissions through her website. She recently wrote her first book: **Painting with Wool,** to rave reviews. Dani travels extensively around the US to well attended workshops teaching her unique methods to enthusiastic attendees.

Advice: Supplies are important. You absolutely need to invest in the right type of wool and supplies for your projects for a good outcome. Don't be afraid to ask questions and connect with the felting community in any way you can.

Selling your work: Whatever you create the most of, and share on social media, that is the type of work that people will request the most of in the form of commissions. Share what you love doing the most.

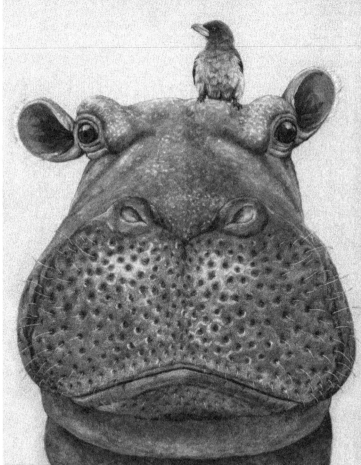

Favorite wools:
MC1 by Living Felt
Maori wool from the Dyeing House Gallery, Italy

Photograph

Felted

85

Materials:
Burlap bag or fabric
Batt: (small amounts) white, dark brown, light brown, tan, peach, orange, dark green, light green, white, yellow, black
Curly or crimped locks: variety of brown and gray - Blue-Faced Leicester sheep locks are a good choice
Pattern, page 100

Lesson 12: 2-D layering to create a feathered look. This wren is more simple to make than he appears. The natural colored wool from the locks, mixed with the batt gives this wren a fluffy feathered appearance without having to create individual feathers.

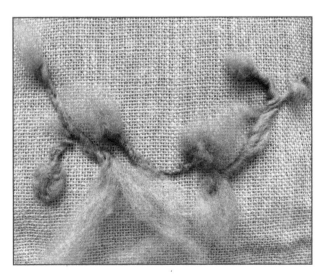

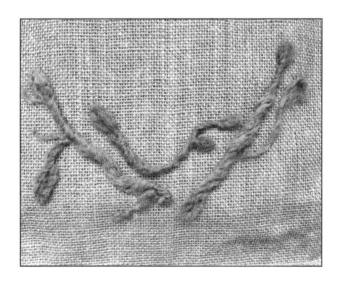

To start your project, make sure the fabric is properly stretched and pinned to your foam pad. If you are working on a bag, put the foam into the bag and felt directly on the bag. Start the vines by twisting strands of dark and light green and felt down as you twist. Leaves are small twists, doubled over, at the ends of the vines.

You can see in this picture how twisting the wool makes a nice, realistic looking vine, as opposed to simply felting down a flat strand of wool. Finish up by tucking in any stray strands.

Trace the bird outline from the pattern onto the fabric and felt down a layer of white batt. The multi tool with #40 needles is great for this task.

Take gray, light and dark brown batt and shade the wren as shown in the picture. The curly locks go on the top after the initial shading. Pick the locks apart a bit and stretch them out a little before felting down. Variegated locks work best as they look the most like feathers.

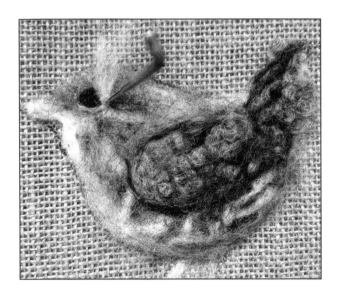

After the shading is done you will begin to outline the wings and tail with the dark brown and black. Make your outlines thin. The eye is a black oval with a white outline.

Begin shading the beak with an initial felt down of peach with a shading of orange. The breast has a very light shade of peach on it.

There are no hard and fast rules in needle felting. Experiment! Have fun! Be willing to take chances with new ideas. Needle felting is a free-form craft. Every lot of wool is slightly different and every persons interpretation of a project is fresh, making your creations completely unique. Enjoy the creative process and don't get hung up on perfectionism. Save the first thing you make, no matter how much you love or hate it and in a few years from now you will look at it and see the amazing progress you've made.

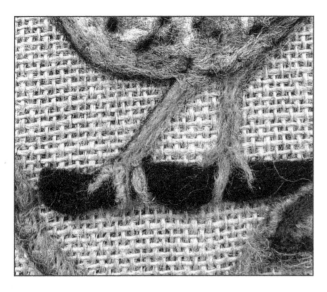

Add a branch in dark brown by twisting and felting down directly to the fabric. The feet get added to the top of the branch and the toes are slightly curled under. The legs and feet are peach with outlines of orange and the edge of the legs have very thick, dark brown outlines.

Add shading to the vines of dark green and yellow. The yellow should be used sparingly.
The flowers are daisy-like. Using your white batt, twist the batt and felt down the petals (reference the 2-D bee landscape for flower instructions).

A full view of the finished wren. Although this is a 2-D piece, do not felt down to hard as it will make this wren overly flat. His feathers should be fluffy.

Tips and Resources

Tips and Hacks from Experienced Felters

Don't ever felt while watching TV! Ouch! Better to listen to podcasts or audio books. A.P.

Use a tray of some type when felting on your lap. Foam pads are not enough, if you miss with the needle and have no tray, it's painful! C.Y.

Invest in good quality supplies, not all wool/kits/needles are created equally and you don't want to be disappointed with something you've spent hours working on because the materials were wrong or of bad quality for the project. J.P.

To get an ultra-smooth piece I trim with scissors then flatten with a very small iron. R.V.

I put an essential oil soaked cotton ball into the middle of my larger projects and felt over it. It repels moths. H.M.

Keep your wool stash (as well as your projects) safely away from pets! My cat had to have surgery because she ate wool and it got lodged in her intestines. L.Y.

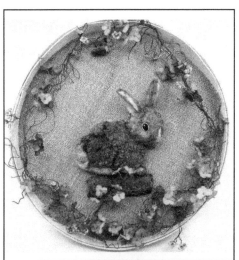

Never store your pieces in a humid environment (basements) as they can absorb musty smells. J.M.

If you are thinking about selling your work, make sure you price it well. Don't undervalue it. I use the formula: cost of the wool + my hourly rate + overhead (fees for selling). M.F.

Making faces and getting measurements right can be very challenging. Take your time and don't felt everything down too tightly until you are sure you have the proportions right. M.A.

Make sure you buy plenty of core wool from a reputable store to start off with. Wool from the big box stores is usually very low grade and hard to use. K.R.

90

Online Groups and Forums

Facebook groups and online forums are huge sources of inspiration and camaraderie. These groups have created a positive and uplifting community for needle felters; for showing off creations to learning new techniques and making new friends. This online community is especially important as there are few local groups to join at this time.

To find online groups, go to Facebook or Google and search under "Needle Felting Groups".

Popular groups:

Needle Felting
Needle Felting UK
Sarafinafeltingfanfare
Living Felt Friends

Storing your wool

Wool is a medium that can be challenging to store and creative thinking is required. It's fluffy, puffy and therefore can be awkward to organize. Other considerations for storage include keeping wool safe from insect infestation and pets (who are attracted to the smell of sheep).

You can approach wool organization in several ways. Most felters store their wool by color but others prefer to do it by breed and processing type. Decisions about storage are usually based on the amount of wool you need to organize. If your collection is small, a simple color system works well but extensive collections require more thought to keep them tidy.

To protect wool from moths and beetles many felters store their wool with cotton balls soaked in essential oils that are known to repel insects. You can also use cedar wood liners or balls. Moth balls are not recommended as they make the wool smell funky. Keeping the wool tightly encased in plastic bags or jars will also keep out the pests.

Always consider pets when storing wool. Animals are very tempted to chew on wool and they will rip apart your wool or projects given a chance. If they swallow the wool it can become lodged in their intestinal tract (which can have disastrous consequences) so keep wool out of reach at all times.

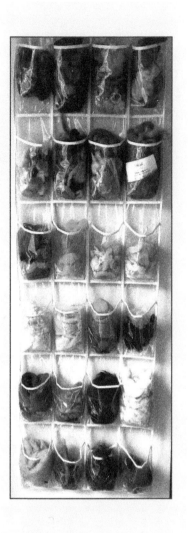

Plastic bins/zip-lock bags
For those who are short on space and need an easily stashable bin system, this is the solution for you. Bins can fit under beds, in closets and can be tucked in wherever you find the room. Bags are optional but a good idea as they keep the bugs out.

Clear plastic shoe organizer
This is a great system for a collection on the small side. The colors are visable and can actually be a part of your decor. This system would not be ideal for someone with pets or that lives in a region with insect issues.

Organization

Plastic stackable bins - This system is great for storing large amounts of wool. You can organize by color/breed/type. Use essential oils and/or cedar wood to repel bugs. If you live in a region with a lot of pests, go the extra mile and encase your wool in zip-lock bags for more protection.

Glass jars are probably the most pet friendly and fool proof way to store wool. Nothing gets in and your wool is completely safe and protected from insect invasion. However, for a large amount of wool, this can be difficult to manage. Also, you need a strong shelf system to hold all the jars. Jars are best for smaller collections.

TIP: If you suspect an insect infestation in your wool, bag it up and put it in the freezer for several weeks. After freezing, take it out and check to see if there are any live insects . Put wool in air tight jars to see if any eggs still hatch, if they do, discard the wool to keep it from infecting the rest of your collection.

Keep your projects away from pets! Wool is an irresistible odor to most dogs and cats.

*Actual photo of teddy bear death and mutilation by pet attack!

Needle Felting Resources

USA

Living Felt

www.livingfelt.com

This friendly company provides a large variety of high quality wool sourced from US farms and is very eco-friendly in their practices.

Sarafina Fiber Art

www.sarafinafiberart.com

Sarafina has a very complete line of high quality fiber and supplies for needle felters along with great kits and tutorials.

The Woolery

www.woolery.com

In business for over 35 years and family owned, they sell fiber to many branches of the fiber arts community.

The Felted Ewe

www.thefeltedewe.com

The Ewe has a good color selection of all types of roving and batt as well as many supplies.

Canada

Fibercraft

www.fibrecraft.ca

Impressive array of fibers and supplies.

Europe

The Makerss

www.themakerss.co.uk

Extensive needle felting wool and supplies for the UK and abroad. Local workshops.

Sweet Pea Dolls

www.sweetpeadolls.co.uk

Inspiring range of fibers, tools and kits. Sweet Pea offers worldwide shipping and is the brand ambassador for Hamanaka, Japan. Nice selection of alternative fibers.

World of Wool

www.worldofwool.co.uk

This company has a huge variety of fiber products and lives up to its name as it delivers worldwide.

Heidi feathers

www.heidifeathers.com

Known for great needles and a nice amount of wool and glass eyes

The Dyeing House Gallery Shop - Italy

A vast assortment of very high quality wool

www.dhgshop.it/promozioniele.php

The Wollknoll Shop - Germany

www.wollknoll.eu/shop/

Local Fiber Sources

Fiber Festivals - There is no other fiber shopping experience that compares to a sheep festival/fair. Farms and producers come from the local region to display their wares and you get to see and feel the wool before buying. Bring lots of money and some large shopping bags with you because the vast amount of wool available is irresistible.

Felting shops that cater primarily to both needle and wet felters are very rare. If you can get to one of these gems make sure you support them! In the US, Sarafina in MD and Living Felt in TX, both have nice sized, well stocked stores and are worth the trip!

Local farms/producers - This is one of the best wool sources of all! Support your local area farms and get to know the people who produce fiber in your area. Wonderful and unique fibers come from small farms.

Local Yarn and Craft shops - Some of these shops carry wool for felters, especially if they cater to spinners. Make sure to call or visit and ask them to start stocking batt and roving if they currently are not. Local shops are usually anxious to cater to the needs of the local fiber population.

Etsy, Amazon and Ebay - Each of these sources has some very good suppliers and many small producers sell on these platforms. Make sure Check reviews carefully before purchasing.

Connect:

Instagram: @naturecrafter

Website: www.naturecrafty.com

Facebook: @naturecrafty - Nature Crafts

Stay in Touch

When new books are released they are offered online to my email subscribers for free or at a very low cost (beta readers) for a limited amount of time. Sign up at:
www.naturecrafty.com

.

If you liked this book, please consider leaving a review. I read each and every review and feel very grateful when readers take the time to leave comments. Thank you in advance!

Lori Rea is an Amazon ranked, best selling author in the arts and crafts genre. A spirited advocate of nature crafting and a self taught needle felter, Lori picked up her first needle and began stabbing wool in 2010. This new passion quickly spiraled into an overabundance of creatures, a tutorial website: NatureCrafty, and her first book, "Needle felting for beginners". A floral designer by trade, with an eye for design, Lori's projects have garnered praise for being beautiful and intricate yet simple to create.

Lori started her crafting journey by spending her childhood summers at her grandmother's art studio in the NYC area. She now finds inspiration from the wilds of the West, where she lives with her husband, son and the occasional mountain lion.

Follow her on Instagram @naturecrafter for current projects and tutorials.

Needle Felting Project

Project Name

Notes

Sketch

Colors

Notes